Your Loss

About the Authors

Christina Ioannidis

Christina is an international speaker, consultant and entrepreneur. Following a varied corporate career in FMCG, Consultancy, Telecoms and IT, she has launched several businesses that have challenged the status quo: always striving to empower women and create business environments that are conducive to diversity and innovation.

She is the founder and CEO of Aquitude, a leading Organizational, People and Market Development Consultancy. Clients include Shell, Barclays, Accenture, Mercer, Detica and PA Consulting.

Christina is also sought-after speaker delivering interactive and engaging keynotes at conferences worldwide. She is a thought leader on the subjects of gender-savvy leadership and talent management, employee and customer engagement, effective product development and marketing, as well as innovation and intrapreneurship. She has been invited to comment on Sky News, The Sunday Times, The Observer, The Evening Standard, The Guardian, among others.

When she is not traveling, Christina enjoys yoga, Pilates and sailing, as well as designing her own jewellery and accessories.

Nicola Walther

Nicola is an ex-Banker turned entrepreneur. Nicola has over 14-years of experience from the world of banking and finance. She has travelled the world in a variety of roles within financial services, including corporate finance, transaction banking and relationship management, culminating in two senior staff roles, firstly within Emerging Markets and, lastly, within Risk at Citi. Nicola has lived, first-hand, numerous of the cultural and structural obstacles that face women in male-dominated fields, such as commercial and investment banking.

During her time at Citi, Nicola co-chaired a Retention & Development Committee for Women in the UK which developed the "Coaching for Success" programme that won external recognition from the Women of the Future Awards. She has devised and actively supported a multitude of Diversity initiatives, only to see the initiatives as "window-dressing"; not changing the underlying issues around stereotyping and structural bias. She is keen to make change happen in the corporate arena, to reduce the stereotyping she has witnessed and redress female bias for the benefit of improved business and, most importantly, for the personal and professional empowerment of women.

Nicola has two children. In her limited spare time she enjoys cooking, dancing and fine dining.

Your Loss

How to win back your female talent

Christina Ioannidis and Nicola Walther

Published by Aquitude Press

Your Loss. How to Win Back Your Female Talent.
© 2010 Christina Ioannidis and Nicola Walther

Cover illustration: Jamel Akib

First published 2010

ISBN 978-0-9567666-0-1

Published by Aquitude Press
Printed in England by Printondemand-worldwide

For Sophie and future generations

Endorsements

"It is time organizations started reviewing diversity metrics as closely as revenue metrics because retaining talent in an environment in which they can perform at their best is what will drive revenues. This book gives a clear framework on how to create such a high-performing and healthy organizational culture." *Vahé Torossian, Corporate Vice President, Microsoft*

"A great guide to more than solving 'the women problem' – this book is all about understanding the motivating factors behind the women who can open doors to a market twice as big as "China and India combined". Surely this is a stat no business can afford to ignore? Ioannidis and Walther provide a blueprint to help all businesses embrace diversity and measure progress against real targets. A must read for all senior management, no matter the size of organisation you lead. " *Carla Stent, Chief Operating Officer, Virgin Management Ltd; Non Executive Director*

"Finally – a practical guide to understanding why and how female talent is lost and, crucially, what can be done to stem the leaking pipeline. With this well-researched and highly readable book, Ioannidis and Walther lead us through the dynamics of change, demonstrating how to stem your losses and build a better, more engaged, profitable and sustainable business for the 21st century." *Cleo Thompson, Writer/Editor, TheGenderBlog.com; formerly of PricewaterhouseCoopers' global gender diversity programme.*

"Turn 'Your Loss' into 'Your Gain' by finding the key ingredients contained in this innovative book. Find out how to put your organisation at the forefront of making women your most valuable asset by reading this book now!" *Anne Watts CBE, Board Member and Co-founder of Women in Banking and Finance*

"A must-read for those running organisations hoping to attract, retain and develop top female talent in our time." *Ellen Miller, Executive Fellow London Business School & former Managing Director, Lehman Brothers*

"Ioannidis and Walther provide critical insight into why women have left corporate positions and how the resulting problem must no longer be considered solely a "woman's issue." Especially for today's sustainability-focused businesses, holistic thinkers – as exemplified by women's ways of leadership – must be identified, encouraged and rewarded. This book can help!" *Andrea Learned, sustainable behavior expert and co-author of "Don't Think Pink: What Really Makes Women Buy – and How To Increase Your Share of This Crucial Market"*

"Keeping and retaining gifted female employees isn't all that hard. First, you have to want to. Second, you have to read this book. No company can compete without having access to the best talent and no company can afford to ignore half the population. What that means is that talent is now a strategic issue which no leader can ignore. Learning how to attract and keep your best women yields endless rewards: it saves money, raises morale and enhances innovation. And that isn't just for women – it's for everyone you employ." *Margaret Heffernan, Author, "Women on Top"*

Contents

Preface

The discussions on gender diversity have, all too often, centered on the "women's issue".

As both corporate and entrepreneurial business women, both Nicola and I have some experience in reading business accounts and profits and losses. It astounded us that the case for creating effective and efficient businesses had not been considered from the enormous losses that the gender-brain drain is generating for corporations.

We calculated that the cost of replacing lost women to an organisation with 20,000 employees could be as much as £200 million. The international consultancy Bain and Co has concluded that if corporations lose 5 percent a year of their talent base for 10 years, then investment in recruitment would need to be increased by 20% in order to keep up with the losses.

These figures just do not add up. Why are corporations still incurring these losses? Why are they losing these women? And where is this lost talent going? We are prime examples of the Lost Women, who have left large business and are forging our futures as entrepreneurs. Figures worldwide show that we are far from alone.

This book is an inside view on the why's of women leaving and how large corporations can create Gender-Savvy cultures to safeguard themselves from losing their top talent. Our research has indicated that this is far from being a gender issue – it is also a generational issue. Corporations should read up or risk being sidelined from their future talent too – the all-important Generation Y coming up the ranks.

This book is not about training. This book is not about learning and development. This book is about how to practically create high-performing and diverse organisations free of blind-spots. It is about keeping the best, most motivated talent who constantly grow and develop whilst contributing to the best of their abilities for their, their employer's and their customers' benefit.

Christina Ioannidis

Acknowledgements

To those who contributed or supported us through the process of forming our ideas and writing the book: Shirley Adrain, Jamel Akib, Alice Avis, Julie Chakraverty, Claire Fedden, Anne Fergusson, Sally Forest, Susan Fuller, Dave Fuller, India Gary, Sarah Gibbs, Will Glendinning, Kate Grussing, Janet Hanson, Georgina Hearson, Debbie Hicks, Sara Hill, Bronwen Horton, Matt Hubbard, Kate Isler, Craig Jones, Carmel Kinloch, Henrietta Kolb, Emily Landis Walker, Friederike Loh, Jesselyn Mah, Colin Maitland, Alison Maitland, Bella Mehta, Maisy Ng, Paul Oddie, Ann Phua, Julia Powell, Vicky Pryce, Sarah Speake, Carla Stent, Cleo Thompson, Axel Walther, Anne Watts, Sharon Williams, and Adeline Yeo. Thank you for your invaluable insights, support and generous advice.

To the twitterers and the networks who spread the word about our quantitative survey: @andrealearned, @Sairee, @vadhwa, 85 Broads, ASTIA, City Women's Network, European Professional Woman's Network, Girl Geek, Heals and Deals, Instituto de Empresa, International Women's Federation of Commerce and Industry (Singapore), Mumpreneurs., Mumsnet, Sister Snog, The International Alliance for Women, The New Zealand Business Woman's Network, Third Door, Women in Technology. Thank you for your ongoing support.

To the women who provided their views on our global survey.

Chapter 1: Introduction

There are three main reasons why organisations must be more vigilant about the female brain drain and find a sustainable solution. The first is that women control the majority of global spending power. The second is that women in senior positions will increase profitability and the third is that governments are legislating on the matter. So far we have seen a great deal of effort made by companies to redress the female brain drain, but with limited results. If organisations are to change effectively they must examine women's motivations, understand the other options open to women and address the issue in a more holistic way.

To understand the issues forcing women to move out of corporate life and resume their careers in entrepreneurial or self-employed environments we spoke to them directly. Some women also run portfolio careers, working for larger businesses as self-employed, while also running entrepreneurial ventures.

We undertook 25 qualitative interviews with senior and executive-level men and women in London, Dubai, Singapore, Melbourne and New York. We also undertook an online survey with 168 women world-wide who gave us their views on:

1. Why women are leaving the security of their full-time jobs, often to become either entrepreneurs or run a portfolio career
2. What the pull factors are that attract women to entrepreneurship
3. Any cultural and structural challenges in the corporate world which make family or caring obligations and career development incompatible
4. What companies can learn from their former female talent to make their cultures more engaging

We listened to the ambitious women who took a scenic route in their careers. Our findings are incorporated in the strategies recommended in this book.

Our research gives clear indications of how organisations can address gender balance. We explain how, by understanding the attraction of entrepreneurship, the micro-level dynamics of a modern career and becoming a Gender-Savvy organisation at a macro level, the exodus of female resources can be reversed.

Achieving gender balance will enable Generation Y (those born in the 80s and 90s) to participate more fully in larger organisations. We find that the next generation of talent (irrespective of gender) reflects very similar motivations and has similar alternative career options to those of the traditional female worker.

The ongoing business case for redressing the 'female brain drain'

1. Women hold the majority of global spending power and earnings potential

'Women now drive the world economy. Globally, they control about $20 trillion in annual consumer spending, and that figure could climb as high as $28 trillion in the next five years. Their $13 trillion in total yearly earnings could reach $18 trillion in the same period. In aggregate, women represent a growth market bigger than China and India combined; more than twice as big, in fact.'[i]

Women are increasingly the prime makers of purchasing decisions. Women account for 83% of all consumer purchases, including everything from cars to healthcare[ii]:

      91% of new homes
      94% home furnishings
      55% consumer electronics
      92% vacations
      80% healthcare
      60% new cars
      89% bank accounts
      93% over-the-counter pharmaceuticals

In the United States, women spend about $7 trillion annually, which equates to over half the US Gross Domestic Product.

Women are now the majority holders of multimillion bank accounts. In the UK, 35% of the population of millionaires is constituted by women. Women millionaires are expected to outnumber their male counterparts by 2020, meaning they will represent 53% of millionaires[iii]. Whether it is through work, outliving their male counterparts or divorce, women are powerful investors and economic contributors.

2. Companies with a record of promoting women are more profitable

According to Catalyst, the leading gender think-tank, the group of companies with the highest representation of women on their top management teams experienced:

> Improved Return on Equity (ROE), at 35.1% higher

> Total Return to Shareholders (TRS) at 34% higher than the groups of companies with the lowest women's representation[iv]

This is echoed in a five-year study at Pepperdine University run by Roy Douglas Adler, which highlights a correlation between high-level female executives and business success. Of the *Fortune* 500 companies, the top 25 companies with cultures supporting women demonstrated 69% higher profitability than the industry median (profit as a percentage of equity). We wholly support the conclusion of the report: 'firms exhibit higher profitability when their top executives make smart decisions. One of the smart decisions those executives have consistently made at successful Fortune 500 firms is to include women in the executive suite so that, regardless of gender, the best brains are available to continue making smart, and profitable, decisions.'[v]

3. Governments are focused on gender balance

In recognition of the powerful impact of women on both corporate profitability and organisational culture, countries around the globe are increasingly putting pressure on their largest public and private institutions to make gender diversity a key component of their corporate governance. In Europe, Norway set the tone by legislating on a 40% quota for women on boards, closely followed by France and it is currently under consideration in Spain.

Australians have gone further: the Australian Stock Exchange has revised its Corporate Governance Principles and Recommendations which require every listed company to disclose its diversity policy. In addition, listed companies have to report on the number of women employees in the whole organisation, in senior management and on the board, while corporate boards will be required to disclose what skills and diversity criteria are sought in any new board appointment. During the writing of this chapter, the UK government announced an enquiry into why there are so few women in boardrooms with the purpose of forming a business strategy to resolve the issue.

Women remain under-served, under-valued and under-represented

The overwhelming conclusion of recent studies is that, despite the improved profile of women in business, women still feel under-served as consumers, and they still leave organisations in disproportionately high numbers at middle management level.

> 'Women feel vastly underserved. Despite the remarkable strides in market power and social position that they have made in the past century, they still appear to be undervalued in the marketplace and underestimated in the workplace. They have too many demands on their time and constantly juggle conflicting priorities—work, home, and family. Few companies have responded to their need for time-saving solutions or for products and services designed specifically for them.'[vi]

While women constitute the majority of university graduates at a global level[vii], and enter the workforce in numbers equal to men, there is a marked absence between middle and senior management.

In our experience, organisations are frequently:

50% women and 50% men at entry level

25% or less women and 75% men in middle management

5% or less women and 95% men at senior or executive leadership level.

As diagram 1 below shows, women manifest a higher level of attrition than men in the mid-career point.

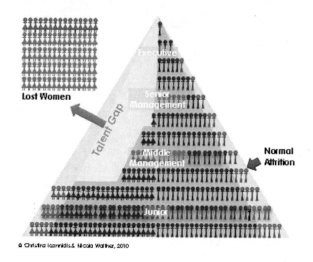

Diagram 1: The Abnormal Attrition Triangle

According to a study by the New York-based Center for Work-Life Policy, women's careers are non-linear; women take a break more often than men. And when they do so, it is for an average of 2.7 years. For every 100 women who take a career break, 89 say they want to get back to work. For every 100 women who take a career break:

> 40 find full-time work
>
> 23 find part-time jobs
>
> 7 become self-employed and
>
> 30 do not return to work[viii]

Women are thus increasingly working part-time after their career breaks, or even leaving corporate life altogether. The exodus is particularly strong when the demands on their time become greater, that is, between the ages of 30 and 40, which is when their work, home and family worlds collide.

We must behave differently if we want a real change

1. Do a better job with the critical factors; pay, promotion, hiring and retention

It sounds obvious, but if organisations want more women in senior positions they need to hire and promote more women into senior roles. This can only be achieved if women are still there when they reach the appropriate levels and if they are taken seriously when they do. We will show in this book how to create a culture which makes women want to stay and enables them to rise through the organisation and qualify for senior roles.

Women still earn less than men. Studies show that, on average, in the US women earn 23% less than men[ix] and in the UK women earn 22% less than men[x]. In a woman's democratic world, this inequity, coupled with a lack of transparency, is an outrage. Fair, equal and transparent remuneration is important because it communicates organisations' egalitarian values. For women, it is not an end in itself. In fact, only 18% of our survey respondents earn more in their new guise than they earned in their corporate lives, suggesting that they didn't leave for financial reasons.

When considering pay, performance-related pay rather than face time, was the recurring theme. As stated by one of the respondents 'Stop insisting on face time and start looking at results'. Payment per se was not the issue – it is the fact that absence is penalised, and so they earn less after having children. Rewarding people transparently, with productivity as the measure, is the way to achieve this.

Transparency and equality in pay are therefore crucial, and go hand in hand with fair promotion and unbiased hiring as the critical factors in retaining women. We do not need to explain how to measure these factors. There are several books on the subject and large organisations are, on the whole, good at measuring whatever they want to measure. However, the fact remains that few firms take a strategic stance towards this matter and the resources for measuring these key factors are not in place. What we cannot emphasise strongly enough is that, if our readers take away one thing from this book, please let it be this:

> *It is essential that the critical factors of pay,*
> *promotion and hiring of women are tracked while*
> *implementing cultural change. Ensure these factors*
> *are accounted for over the long term in the same*
> *way as net profits are.*

These are the factors with which to gauge achievement of the strategic goal. As mentioned above, organisations which are not tracking these factors already will be found lacking when governments oblige them to publish the information (as we expect they will in the UK) as part of their legal publication of annual reports.

2. Understand the dynamics of where women go and why

We discuss, in Chapter 3, a model allowing cultural change. Step One is to accept and understand the problem. We interviewed and surveyed highly successful women who chose to leave large organisations, and we asked them why they left. Below we give an overview of where they go and what can be learned from their new ventures. Many of them have become entrepreneurs.

We have entered a new era of economic participation, with women in the driving seat. On a global level, in recent years, there has been a significant rise in female entrepreneurship. In the US, the number of firms owned by women grew by 19.8% between 1997 and 2002, and then to 55% after 2002. Today, 10.1 million firms in the US are owned by women. In China women are becoming entrepreneurs at the rate of 13%, in Brazil at a rate of 2.7%[xi].

In the UK, female-only start-ups increased by 9% in 2008 (in absolute figures there were 90,000 start-ups in 2008 against 83,000 in 2007[xii]). This may be compared with an increase in male-owned start-ups of no more than 1% in 2008. The most entrepreneurial age group for females is 35-44[xiii].

We believe that women are voting with their stilettos. While the typically expressed view is that women are leaving their professional careers and 'going off to have children', this could not be further from the truth. Women are doing what we call side-ramping: re-entering the labour market as entrepreneurs.

Dr Kim Peters, Professor Michelle Ryan, and Professor Alex Haslam from the University of Exeter have undertaken many experiments on the subject of career ambition. They present evidence that women express lower career ambition and are more likely to opt out of their careers than their male colleagues. However, they say that a 'very important determinant' of people's career ambition is their perception of how they fit in with an organisation and with its leadership. Evidence from surveys and experiments conducted with a range of professions, including medicine and the police, shows that where women perceive that they do not fit in with leaders in their field, they have lower levels of career ambition, and a greater desire to opt out from their careers'.[xiv]

3. Learn from the entrepreneurs

It is important for organisations, senior leaders, corporate boards and shareholders to understand the structural issues hampering the development of women in their corporations. These, in turn, affect their capability to deliver product and service propositions which cater for the demanding female customer.

We believe that corporations need to reframe their approach to talent management and to treat female employees as they would deal with their toughest customers. This kind of shift in mind-set will result in greater employee loyalty, reduced female employee attrition and create a loyal customer-base and a powerful marketing voice. Certainly, entrepreneurial businesses are achieving this, and this is one area where big companies can learn from their smaller counterparts.

The main reasons cited by our interviewees and survey respondents for turning towards entrepreneurship were:

Fulfilment

Entrepreneurship gives women channels for fulfilment currently not available in the inherited business structures of traditional organisations. These organisations grew up with a command-and-control ethos. Since the Industrial Revolution the workforce has been seen as a cost and, consequently, managed as one. Women stepping away wanted more autonomy and freedom. They wanted to feel passionate about their jobs in a way that the traditional control culture doesn't allow. It is evident from literature and from our research that this is a more important factor for women than for men, particularly when considering the fact that in most cases there is a cost (childcare) associated with the woman returning to the workforce. We cover this in chapter 2, which is about how to harness passion in the workplace.

Flexibility

Entrepreneurship allows flexibility in working practice. Although each interviewee emphasised that entrepreneurship is not for the work-shy, they all expressed an appreciation of flexibility in working hours. Flexibility is often associated with part-time working and we have observed it is one of the major areas of negative stereotyping in the large organisations.

> 54% of women start a business so they can choose what hours they work (compared with only 35% of men)[xv].

> 21% of women give family commitments as a reason for becoming self-employed (compared with only 2% of men)[xvi].

We cover this topic, including the non-linear nature of modern careers, in chapter 3.

Innovation

Entrepreneurship gave them an opportunity to realise a dream. We discuss how to achieve this in chapter 4. There are several firms who have successfully converted this aspiration into an opportunity for employee retention and ownership of new intellectual property.

Technology

Technology, specifically the Internet, has made entrepreneurship a better proposition than it was a few years ago. Now anyone can set up a business overnight and begin to generate revenue within a short time. Organisations are not just competing with a shrinking talent pool but also with the attractions of entrepreneurship.

It is interesting to note that female entrepreneurs are more likely than their male counterparts to use technology in their products or services. They are also more likely to offer a product or service unfamiliar to the markets, to have fewer competitors, and more likely too than male businesses to be offering a product or service developed in the last year[xvii] to the market. Women's innovative capacity is increasingly visible. So, how can this latent innovatory talent be harnessed to create the lean, flexible, innovative organisation which will give current and future employees the cutting edge?

Freedom

Women and ethnic minorities once excluded or segregated from the corporate world are being drawn into the labour market, owing to financial and social shifts, as well as by individual liberation. However, their values and working practices are not in tune with the old-style, monolithic approach of traditional business. Women of mixed ethnicity, it has been observed, are over two and a half times more entrepreneurial than white women[xviii].

To build both the gender and the ethnic diversity in organisations, exploitation of individual motivation for fulfilment with entrepreneurship needs to be considered. How can the benefits and fulfilment of independence be offered?

Ease

The credit crunch has increased the speed with which would-be entrepreneurs can set up shop. Entrepreneurs can visit entrepreneurial resource groups and, after one breakfast meeting, can have their web designers, accountants, coaches, extended sales-forces and potential customers ready for action.

Existing organisations have a built-in advantage because entrepreneurship is certainly not an easy option and requires tenacity and confidence as well as the right skill-set. However, the best talent has these qualities, and the changes described above have helped its way into the entrepreneurial world. Companies have to wake up to the fact that entrepreneurship is now a more attractive proposition for the top talent than ever before. Large organisations are pulling out all the stops to attract the best human capital, but so is entrepreneurship. Whether it is social, not-for-profit or for-profit, entrepreneurship represents an opportunity for highly skilled talent to make a difference, while doing something it cares about too.

4. Understand the female context at a micro level

Organisations should understand women's priorities, represented by work, home and family. These three areas of life were formerly distinct and separate. However, with today's collaborative, web-based technology, women, and Generation Y, exist where the three worlds coincide.. The Internet, and Facebook in particular, is where these two population groups communicate with their professional, social and family circles simultaneously. Corporate culture needs to embrace this seamlessness.

We believe there are structural challenges preventing women from maximising their performance and purchasing power. These challenges have evolved from assumptions, or stereotyping, fostered in organisations, departments and even nationally, in some cases, about women and how they can best perform their roles as professionals, consumers and nurturers.

Once women cease being 'undervalued in the marketplace' and 'underestimated in the workplace'[xix], and are reassured about their positive contribution to both, they will unleash their economic power.

Women themselves know how to overcome the impasse of the three key roles of professional, consumer and nurturer. To create goods and provide services which will attract the women's economy, organisations must encourage a strong female talent base, responsible for their design and delivery, and adopt working practices which will retain women at all levels.

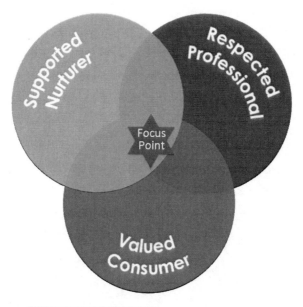

Diagram 2: The Gender-Savvy Focus Point

5. Change corporate culture on a macro level

We like to think of men and women as the *yin* and the *yang* of business. Both women and men bring positive attributes to business and each is needed, as with the *yin* and the *yang*, to achieve balance and optimum performance.

Until now, corporations have taken a sticking plaster approach – focusing on 'fixing' women. The gender diversity discussion is thus in danger of being seen as no more or less than positive discrimination. Activities intended to promote women have actually served to sideline them even further[xx].

Wholesale culture change requires a strategic focus:

> Diversity must be the responsibility at the highest levels of senior management, not at the 'necessary evil' level of Human Resources.

> Diversity must be made central to the business and measured against real, consistent targets.

Google, a young and progressive organisation, does not experience this phenomenon of women leaving because these cultural characteristics were embedded at the outset. They are rewarded with benefits visible and palpable to both genders, with a working culture that is inclusive, flexible and, most importantly, high-performing.

Become a Gender-Savvy organisation

Having looked at the motivations leading women into entrepreneurship above, and how organisations can change their own perspectives at all levels to prepare for change, we have developed a system of Gender-Savvy Elements to engender a culture attractive to women as customers *and* employees.

Cultural Elements of a Gender Savvy Organisation			
PASSION	FLEXIBILITY	COLLABORATION	SUSTAINABILITY
Fire	Water	Air	Earth

© Christina Ioannidis & Nicola Walther, 2010

Diagram 3: The Gender-Savvy Cultural Elements

Each of the following chapters focuses on one of the elements of our model, Passion, Flexibility, Innovative Collaboration and Sustainability. We then go on, in Part Two of the book, to offer practical solutions using the model, in marketing to women and in managing women. Finally, we offer the women practical advice about what they can do for themselves to encourage change.

We are not advocates of a female-centric system of talent management. We believe in a balanced system, one which prepares for the influx into the workforce of the far more demanding Generation Y. Modern careers differ in direction as well as in the effect of individual and social pressures. We have created the Gender-Savvy model to read the mind and the motivations of the toughest and, potentially, most loyal employees.

If organisations want to stem this brain drain and save the millions invested in grooming and developing women, as well as attracting the best new talent, they should consider business culture strategically and beyond diversity.

Section 1: Gender-Savvy Cultural Elements

Chapter 2: Passion

'The master of the art of living makes little distinction between his work and his play, his labour and his leisure, his mind and his body, his education and his recreation, his love and his religion. He simply pursues his vision of excellence in whatever he does, leaving others to decide whether he is working or playing. To him, he is always doing both.' Chinese Taoist philosopher Lao-Dzu[xxi]

This quotation was on the office wall of one of the most passionate leaders we have ever come across. He ran the most successful business in his area of banking. It is also quoted in Tina Seelig's book, *What I Wish I Knew When I Was 20*. She says that a mark of true success is finding a career in which you can't believe people actually pay you to do your job. The truth is, we work harder at things we are passionate about.

What do we mean by passion, and why is it important?

When you are passionate about something time just runs away with you

We believe that society has developed a false view of passion, that it is a flaming, burning emotion. Those employees who claim to have no passion in their work should be encouraged to consider what they are doing when time runs away with them. Some people are not the stereotypical, hyper-enthusiastic 'skip down the corridor' types, but they will quietly spend time doing what they love.

We are no longer in the immediately post-Industrial Revolution world, where the word 'passion' in relation to work was anathema. Work is no longer a '9-to-5' phenomenon where employees are expected to work as automatons. Taylorism gave us the production line, with each worker performing a specific task and any emotional attachment to the performance of the task was irrelevant. Young people today are reading Tina Seelig's book (she is a professor at Stanford University where it is required reading for the Innovation class) and they are taught that their career should harness their passion. This has been true for women for many years, as they have made difficult choices in their work-life balance.

In today's corporate world passion is a key business imperative. People's hearts need to be in what they are doing in order to feel motivated. People working with passion will give you access to productivity through discretionary effort beyond anything money or extra headcount can buy. One of our entrepreneurs said in her interview, '...if you are really passionate about what you do it doesn't matter what time you are working at, you just do it. If we're working at 1 a.m. or 2 a.m. on a Sunday then that's OK because we are doing what we want to do.' *Adeline Yeo, former Advertising Executive turned social entrepreneur.*

People, and especially women, quit when they lose passion for what they are doing

'I decided that I wasn't going to stay in a role where I felt zero passion. I felt that my heart was dying and I felt I was waking up in the morning just to go to work to pay bills. It really wasn't what I wanted to do in my life. I realised that you can carry on doing this because it's safe and secure and you get the salary, or you make the courageous decision and you quit and go out into the unknown. So that's what I did. I had no idea what I wanted to do. I wasn't quitting to start my own business or to be an entrepreneur. I was quitting because I was no longer being authentic to myself, and I was no longer passionate about my work and my heart just felt like it was dying.' *Sally Forrest, former Boots plc executive, turned entrepreneur.*

If they are not understood as individuals and for what they want from their careers, they will take their experience, skills and intelligence and leave. As stated in the introduction, fulfilment was emphasised as a key reason why our interviewees and survey-participants moved away from the corporate environment towards entrepreneurship. Research shows that women are more likely to leave in circumstances where they do not feel passionate about their job.

According to research by Henig and Jardim in their book *The Managerial Woman*[xxii], women appear to have a greater sense of fulfilment from a career and a strong sense of 'being' in a job. Fulfilment is largely attributed to their personal development. By contrast, for men, a job is perceived as an activity which is rewarded by moving up the career ladder which is also best compensated by monetary means.

The Hidden Brain Drain Task Force, the flagship project for the Center for Work-Life Policy, reflects this in its ground-breaking research. 'When asked what they want out of work, highly qualified women (in contrast to highly qualified men) emphasize non-monetary rewards. For women, five drivers or types of motivation (high quality colleagues, flexible work arrangements, collaborative teams, give back to society, recognition) trump the size of the paycheck'[xxiii].

One pertinent example of a failure to motivate through passion is the industry which has suffered most from female brain-drain, banking and finance. According to the Center for Work-Life Policy, in this industry 'the push factors (for women) outweigh pull factors, with failure to find a career either satisfying or enjoyable as the dominant trigger for leaving.'[xxiv]

Engaging with Passion

Our interviewees and survey respondents consistently used the words below in relation to passion:

> Communication
> Belief in the leader
> Authentic Behaviour
> Employee Engagement
> Clear goals
> Structured objectives
> Ownership

However, these elements are expressed differently by the genders. Reading this chapter, bear in mind the table below showing typical behaviours and association difference by gender:

Preferences	Male	Female
Communication	Direct	Indirect
Belief in Leader	Primarily rank	Primarily actions
Authentic Behaviour	Expectations must be met	Won by 'Walking the Talk'
Employee Engagement	Ad hoc	Long-term, reviewed
Structured objectives	Clear structured communication	
Ownership	Individual	Collegial

Table 1: Typical behaviours by gender

Passionate leadership means showing your own passion

It may seem obvious because it is such a basic management principle, but employees want to see and believe in the vision from the leadership. They want authentic passion, which requires positive energy and belief from the leader.

Commenting on the success of The Sanctuary Spa, CEO Alice Avis said, 'The Sanctuary had a clearly communicated vision of doing something for the greater good. Inspirational leadership is not rocket science. YOU have to genuinely believe it. With the Sanctuary it was about women for women and we all had enthusiasm and energy.'

The passion was clearly communicated by the leader. She was behaving in an authentic and consistent manner. She engaged the employees and they felt that they owned and were part of a mission.

Communication takes time. One of our interviewees described her leader as being, '…absolutely passionate, he absolutely loves his staff and is utterly supportive of us. I don't know how he finds so much time for his staff and his clients but he gives his all, one hundred per cent of the time'. She said, 'and I would walk over hot coals for him. If he asked me to do anything I would do it for him as he absolutely deserves it.' This manager is described has having made a huge difference to the energy of the business and has made his own firm the undisputed leader in the market place, simply by taking his own passion and harnessing the business to it. He has developed an acronym, HEAT, hunger, engagement, anticipation and talent.

Managers should ask themselves: Are you and your leaders doing this as a routine activity? Would your staff say these things about you? If not, what can you do today to change this?

Ask the employees what they want

Employee engagement should be an open dialogue. When asked what corporations could do to retain high-quality women, our survey respondents repeatedly made comments such as, 'Talk to them regularly about what they're looking for, really listen and be willing to act on what you hear. ...Be thinking about what the right next step/role for her is ahead of time, rather than having to drum up something in a hurry when she says she's leaving.'

An effective example of this was given to us in one of our interviews:

'I was working for a leading bank which ran an employee opinion survey. Sometimes the results were hard to interpret. The management decided to look at the key issues affecting results that were significantly better or worse than the previous year. Focus groups, using volunteers, were asked leading questions about the real issues, "When you said this what did you actually mean?" They ran the groups using facilitators allowing the employees to feel comfortable saying what they liked. They found that the volunteers in the focus groups were genuine in their concerns and their feedback. The feedback was presented to senior management, who then worked specifically on addressing the issues. Some of the ideas raised made the management slightly nervous, but armed with the feedback about what the employees wanted they were able to communicate clearly in addressing issues raised. The success of this clear communication, specifically addressing the issues raised by employee groups, was measurable. Even in a year when there were significant numbers of redundancies, the employee feedback in the next survey improved.' *Shirley Adrain, former banker.*

Enable them to do the job well by providing the best conditions

Peter Senge, author of *The Fifth Discipline*, emphasises that employees must be provided with conditions which will allow them to give their best and their customers to receive it. Constant review of the implementation of technology, of a sympathetic environment for innovation and transformational collaborations (more of these in Chapter 4) is essential for maintaining motivation among the best and brightest.

A colleague of ours was opening a new business account at one of the UK's high street banks recently. The account manager was excited about winning the new business and began the paperwork. However, a process which should have taken 20 minutes with the right technology, took over two hours because the forms to be completed were filed on a centrally-held Excel spreadsheet. The system kept crashing and the account manager was embarrassed about having such antiquated technology. The bank was about to close for the day and, anxious about the delay, the account manager didn't have time to check the answers fully before submission. There was a small error on the spreadsheet and the account, which the account manager had stayed behind to work on after hours, was not opened for two weeks. The staff member is now demotivated and the customer unhappy. The passion for new business is dead.

Several of our interviewees talked about speed of change, being able to use new technology and working conditions which are more inviting as reasons for walking away from large corporations. Our advice when engaging with employees is to ask how they would like to change things. We asked the bank employee in the example above what he would do (given that every account manager in the country uses this system and experiences similar difficulties) and he had many good and economically sound ideas. Had senior management at his bank addressed this issue by approaching employees and had they been prepared to invest in the appropriate technology, they may have solved this problem.

Focus on strengths to achieve excellence, rather than on weaknesses which achieve, at best, mediocrity

The old philosophy of management revolved around perfection: employees had to be excellent at everything and had to attend skills-development programmes to improve weak areas. This philosophy is no longer relevant. Everyone is good at something: if they love it, they will do it well and with persistence. If you enjoy your work, perfecting your skills will be more enjoyable and, most importantly, will come naturally.

'… to leverage passion in the corporate world, you have to find out what people enjoy doing, and get them doing it. It's as though we are conditioned the wrong way. If you have a child at school and they come back with a school report, a normal parent will look at it and say, he got 'A' for this, 'B' for this, 'C' for maths —oh, maths isn't very good, we need to get you some more help in maths. And a lot of corporations do this. We do the strength-weakness opportunities thing for individuals and then we focus on the weak end. But really what we should be doing is focusing on what they are good at. Actually you should ignore the weakness. If you've got somebody who's good at sales, then you focus on giving them roles in sales because that is what they are passionate about.' *Sally Forrest*

Organisational tools which encourage passionate engagement

There are a number of techniques we recommend for harnessing this engagement with passion. Most of them require continual involvement from leaders and dialogue with employees, which is what we heard consistently from our interviewees.

'I think it's about getting leaders to be leaders and getting leaders to engage with their people. Talent management should be owned individually by all leaders. It's not for advisers to come in every six months, run a workshop and then disappear again. It's a constant thing and not actually rocket science. It's about leaders taking ownership for engagement with their people and embedding that concept into organisations.' *Matt Hubbard, Head of HR for Corporate Banking, Lloyds Banking Group*

Integrate ways of working that allow for continual engagement

Women are particularly guided by a desire to grow and learn. Continual learning goes beyond traditional training, which is most often a solitary intervention on the back of a 'need' highlighted by an external stakeholder, e.g., the line manager. This is not about 'fixing' women.

We believe that to create a culture of continual learning and development, it has to be undertaken in real-life business scenarios, supported by constant reviews, coaching and personal growth programmes. This is the development which women appreciate most. Three examples of adapting training in a context-based approach are:

Shadowing techniques

Shadowing a student is one of the most powerful learning techniques because the coach or mentor is able to provide the employee with tangible feedback and targeted advice for learning.

One of our interviewees has a number of mentees. She watches them in meetings, seeing how they gain executive presence. She watches them at work and advises them. She says that training courses can teach various techniques, for example, but only in a real environment can the effect of their application be seen.

Coaching with targeted training and development plans

At Citi, the Coaching for Success Programme for Women brought a series of normally individual courses together, in addition to mentoring from a senior in another area of the bank over a six-month period. The same group of women from across the bank's community was brought together once a month for a training day (e.g., Goal-Setting, Personal Profiling, Communication Skills). The bond the group formed gave the training days more relevance and allowed for discussion later about how the training affected daily and monthly reality. Promotion rates among this group improved substantially.

Internal Mentoring Meshes

The term 'the old boy network' is often aired in discussions about the challenges facing female advancement in business. It is defined as, 'An informal, exclusive system of mutual assistance and friendship through which men belonging to a particular group, such as the alumni of a school, exchange favors and connections, as in politics or business'[xxv]. In an environment dominated by between 75% and 95% men, the middle to senior management ranks in business seem out of reach for women, and so the gnarled existence of 'the old boy network' is a reality for women in business.

The recent Off-Ramps, On-Ramps research supports this. Women emphasise that they lack support from senior colleagues: 89% don't have a sponsor to move them forward in their careers, 68% lack mentors and 61% lack role-models.[xxvi]

There are unwritten rules of male camaraderie which, rather than being malicious, are only natural – as humans, we are programmed to stick to 'our own kind' and so women do not have the same appeal in business because they generally act, think and behave very differently from their male counterparts. This is, once again, the reason for educating employees at every level on how these gender differences affect behaviour, business practices and overall performance.

In an organisation built on a culture of inclusiveness and openness, it is important to encourage employees to network strategically and across the gender divide. For silos to break in businesses they need to be injected with the views of different individuals.

'I think it's less about a men's club than that it's not conducive to a diverse club', *Kate Isler, Senior Director Windows Consumer Marketing, Microsoft*

Some organisations have instituted mentoring programmes but they tend to focus on single relationships between male and female executives. We believe it is necessary to build on a number of these networking frameworks to create their individual living, changing, growing Mentoring Mesh. We define the Mentoring Mesh as a suite of mentoring relationships critical for both personal and professional development, in short, an individual's board of directors. To encourage employees to develop these relationships, organisations need to:

> Demonstrate to employees the importance of maintaining their visibility

> Coach employees to crystallise their mentoring objectives

> Support employees in creating their own Mentoring Mesh within, and very importantly, outside the company and the industry. Diversity in mentor-types is also critical to cross-fertilise ideas, learning and opportunities across sectors

> Introduce techniques for sustaining the multiple relationships so that objectives are kept in sight

Engagement champions – set the employees' passion gauge

An Engagement Champion is a senior member from a business who mentors a junior employee on their fulfilment levels. This champion is not to be confused with the employee's business mentors, who are still a valuable resource in developing what the junior employee has learned from experience and generally 'opening their horizons' within the business. The Engagement Champion is responsible for dialogue with the individual and tailors the role, responsibilities, and even the career path of the individual employee, always from the point of view of the employee's fulfilment.

An Engagement Champion needs to be integrated in the Talent Management process rather than peripheral, and be involved in the individual Personal Development Plans (PDP) planning and reviews. We would even go as far as to suggest that these sessions be called Personal Engagement Planning.

'If the people that you work with believe in you it actually refuels the passion' *Jesselyn Nah, former IT consultant now CEO of a software development company*

Women tend to associate a stronger sense of fulfilment with their intellect (in terms of learning) and being involved in their work. Organisational strategy and implementation processes have to be aligned, and the organisation must consistently deliver on coaching, identifying and ensuring passion on a daily basis. This is why the Engagement Champion is a key figure, helping to keep employee passion alive.

Learn from entrepreneurs through Peer and Reverse Mentoring

Our research into what drives women to leave corporations to become entrepreneurs highlighted a strong belief by the female respondents that to enable culture change, corporations have to learn from entrepreneurs.

One of our respondents commented, when asked what companies can do to harness the passions of its employees: 'Companies need to be more entrepreneurial, that is provide more employee empowerment within the framework and guidelines of the company.'

Respondents were particular about areas in which large organisations can learn from entrepreneurs. These include:

> Flexibility of working
>
> Freedom of ideas
>
> Space: both in terms of autonomy and physical work-space
>
> Reporting: the frequency and need to report to line management, with an implied lack of trust

'Have the confidence to believe in the skills of the talent within an organisation, learn to truly empower and create an environment that enables people to deliver and maintain a level of control over their work-life balance.' *Survey respondent*

As mentioned above, training and development traditionally employs single sessions intended for rapid, concentrated teaching. However, our brain learns through experience. We have devised an experience-based learning programme designed to cross-fertilise skills, experience and learning between professionals in large corporations and entrepreneurs.

As David Clutterbuck, one of the UK's greatest authorities on mentoring, maintains, 'Whenever any two people come together in a learning relationship, they bring a whole spectrum of different experiences, some of which may be valuable to the other person. When one party is felt to be in some sense superior, the sense of mutual exploration and discovery is muted…Abandoning status and authority within a relationship not only makes for greater rapport and openness, it also influences in a very positive way the quality of the learning dialogue.[xxvii]'

Mixing them offers the opportunity for entrepreneurs and corporate talent to learn from each other and is an invaluable resource for the personal development needs of top talent. Both the entrepreneur and the corporate professional mentor each other for a predetermined time with pre-agreed aims. Both parties benefit from the equal interaction. It is intended to be a helpful relationship based upon mutual trust and respect. It is less a formal professional relationship than a structured learning partnership.

These programmes enable both:

>peer-mentoring: where a difference in age or tenure of the individuals is not critical, but they can benefit from each other's diverse experiences

>reverse mentoring: where age may be a factor, whereby the younger of the two can offer learning to the older, more experienced mentor (and vice versa)

For example, in one of the peer-mentoring relationships between an internet entrepreneur and a female investment banker, the banker was able to advise the entrepreneur on how to market their product to the financial services market, particularly advising on the key risk concerns of their technology. The investment banker was able to learn from the entrepreneur on matters relating to personal transitions and change management which she was able to put into practice in a time of great personal transition within the bank.

Lack of profit-and-loss experience is one of the biggest obstacles for senior women in business. Women are often found in support functions of the business, HR, Marketing, Legal. They are seldom involved in the running of a business unit or a product line. It is assumed they do not have this experience so the boardroom door stays firmly closed. Organisations can benefit from the implementation of such a programme to enable women to obtain profit-and-loss responsibility by experiencing the context and challenges of the entrepreneurial business.

As a senior banker commented, 'Banking and financial services are very similar in that there are no women on boards and there are very few women running departments. Formal career planning is really important. It's something that I tried to initiate when I was diversity champion. The issue was that line managers sit down and they say "Who shall we promote? Yeah let's put X on the shortlist (but actually in the end we'll promote someone else but we felt really good about ourselves because we had a diverse shortlist)." When actually those people have no intention of promoting a woman because in their mind, "Oh well she doesn't have the gravitas, she's never chaired anything, she's never run a frontline Profit and Loss…" It's not a woman thing, it's just that big companies don't tend to do any formal career planning and I think that is critical if you are going to get women into the senior ranks…'

As we shall see in Chapter 3, understanding diversity is about appreciating others' perspectives. If a predominantly (male) middle management is to learn what women need in the corporate environment, a facilitated mutual mentoring programme between a female entrepreneur who has left the corporate world and a male executive (still within it) will enable the latter to understand from her first-hand experience the desirable business culture and working practices that women seek. This learning can be built upon and mentors can formulate plans for reviewing the business culture and working practices to help retain women.

Use behavioural profiling in the hiring process

The best employers should move beyond purely gender-based distinctions and understand what motivates the individual. The Language and Behavioural Profile is a powerful research-backed profiling tool to identify individual motivation triggers. When hiring and restructuring such profiling helps organisations hire the right person for the job by matching drivers to the role. In this way the organisation ensures that the employee, its critical asset, is doing what is best suited to him or her. The employee appreciates that the organisation cares enough to ensure that he or she attains the highest sense of fulfilment and satisfaction by performing activities they enjoy.

As one of our respondents said, 'Conversation established passions. Spend more one-to-one time to actually find out what make that person tick.' We believe that this acts as a message of authenticity from the organisation. It enables employees to make their contributions in ways meaningful to them and make them perform more than merely what is expected of them.

Conclusion

Passion is central to business in terms of retaining the best talent and achieving the best results. This is particularly important for women. Engaging with passion requires clear and continuous communication and an ongoing commitment from senior management to provide the best possible working conditions. Women in particular fuel their passion through personal growth. Their engagement can be enhanced by developing strong coaching and mentoring programmes within the business and outside through relationships with entrepreneurs.

.

Chapter 3: Flexibility

Ricardo Semler, CEO of Brazil's fastest growing company states, 'I've learnt that any adult welcomes freedom, flexibility and responsibility if it increases the gratification he gets from what he does for a living'[xxviii].

Flexibility and stereotypes

Discussions on flexibility tend to be reduced to a stereotypical view of a mother who works part-time and so is assumed to be unambitious. It is assumed that she no longer takes her career seriously and she comes to work as more of a hobby.

An example of this change in attitude was highlighted in our interviews. One of our interviewees said that, following the birth of her child, her previously unquestioned and highly productive arrangement of a day-a-week working from home suddenly came under scrutiny. People would use air quotes when saying 'working from home' and exclude her on critical calls, as if she were using it as an excuse for a day off.

Another of our interviewees in a high-profile position suggested to her husband that perhaps he could work part-time while the children were young in order to balance parenting time. His immediate response was, 'I couldn't possibly do that, I wouldn't be taken seriously ever again'.

It is true that many women request reduced or flexi-time schedules to balance work and family (66% of the Work-Life Policy respondents[xxix]), but the common prejudices against this should be removed so as not to stunt their professional development. A flexible work schedule should not mean the end of a career.

Society already places a great deal of pressure on women: as discussed in Chapter 1, women are in the driving seat of family expenditure, family organisation, and other caring responsibilities. On average, European women continue to devote twice as much time as men do to domestic tasks: 4 hours, 29 minutes a day, compared with 2 hours, 18 minutes for men[xxx]. Not only do women have to weigh their sense of professional responsibility with their guilt in leaving children at nursery or with a nanny, they also have to live up to what is expected of them in managing a household and a career, and negative stereotyping when they are at work. Until it is no longer expected that a woman always has the main responsibility for children and household, we will never find balance in the workplace.

Nicola Walther, one of the authors of this book, said, 'I used to joke that I was a Director at Citi and that I was also CEO of my household (my husband being Chairman, non-exec). My husband does far more than many others I know, but it still isn't the same as having a stay-at-home wife to manage the household for you.'

Broaden perspectives on flexibility in the workplace

Flexibility comes in many forms:

> Working hours
> Range of responsibilities
> Linearity of the career
> Range and wealth of experience
> Management reporting

These examples of flexibility affect measurement of individual performance and need to be managed with discretion and in their own terms. Managers should be wary of examining successful performance through their own cultural lens. To embrace true flexibility in an organisation entrenched views about gender and flexibility have to be modified.

How to achieve this cultural change is to give employees responsibility for their own careers. Why should advancement and ambition be in a straight line on a graph, with a plateau at the top? Why can't it have kinks and spurts or shifts across disciplines, according to what suits the individual? We live in a colourful world, and success does not require a straight line. All the individuals, whose careers are depicted in our diagrams opposite, are highly successful.

Individual 1 may have a traditional path with 10 years' part-time work while children are preschoolers

Individual 2 may be a high-flyer who leaves a large corporation to start her own business which is then bought by a corporation

Individual 3 may be a mother who decides to start her own business and then returns to the corporate world and

Individual 4 may be an entrepreneur who takes up a series of board positions following successful IPO of her own business

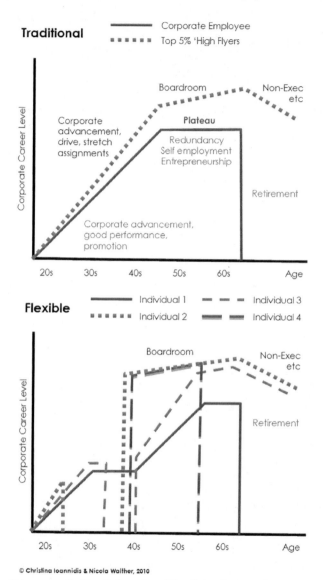

© Christina Ioannidis & Nicola Walther, 2010

Diagram 3: Traditional vs Flexible Career Paths

Flexible organisations ensure that employees are empowered to choose when to increase or decrease their professional responsibilities based on their availability and life stage. Not only does this retain excellent employees, it harnesses their passion for work by giving them the autonomy we discussed in Chapter 2.

If you consider the motivations for women setting up their own businesses you will find that they have not left their passion for working behind just because they want flexibility. We found three critical factors present in all of our female entrepreneurs:

>   An undying willingness to work and be challenged

>   A preparedness to work 24/7 to create, develop and grow a (new) business

>   A need to achieve fulfilment on their own terms

So, how can a company exploit this innate need for personal fulfilment and growth based on passion and the need to contribute and broaden the corporate perspective on flexibility?

Decentralise employee work-scope: assign project work rather than applying the traditional functional-based role descriptions

Empower: enable employees to have freedom to recommend changes in their own career trajectory. This is where the Engagement Champion is key.

Support a mind-set of 'difference' and change, and foster intrapreneurs (corporate entrepreneurs): allocate a percentage of time on innovation or 'focus on other stuff' (more of this in Chapter 4).

Why don't entrepreneurs worry about whether they are fully engaged in their jobs? Quite simply, they love what they do! They are living their dream, which combines the power of flexibility and creativity. Flexibility gives freedom to make choices on how to work, where to work, and what to do. This flies in the face of the traditional working culture, where presenteeism rules.

Adeline Yeo, a Singaporean social entrepreneur states that the appeals of entrepreneurship over her previous career in PR stems from, 'Having freedom of all my time. Being able to make decisions. I'm a very confident person so if I don't like how something is done then suddenly I get really itchy. When I was working in a corporation I couldn't say anything that would affect things but now I can.'

Box 1: Flexibility Case Study

As Kate Grussing, a leading headhunter in the UK advises corporations to have 'more flexible career paths where companies can give individuals opportunities to try different skills or functions or geographies. One way of doing that, certainly that I've seen more in this environment [the recession], is companies giving individuals sabbaticals. The individual may or may not come back but the odds are that it will be a good thing for that company and for the individual if you take a long-term view. It could be to go and do a PhD, it could be to go and do volunteer service, or it could be to develop a business plan for something that that individual has always sought. I think too often the professionals that I know think that if they put their hand up to do something like that it's the end of the road rather than opening new doors. I think that is the thing that would have the greatest single impact because people have these sorts of entrepreneurial urges at all different stages of their career.'

Kate gave an example of flexibility in career path, which allowed an employee to stretch herself: 'I can think of a good friend who is now a client who rose through the ranks at (an American bank) as a salesperson. She moved to one of their biggest competitors. It was really a lateral move, again as a salesperson. At the competitor they encouraged her to move into a senior HR role, even though she had never worked in HR. I think if she had still been at her previous employer, they would not have thought of her for that role. She certainly wouldn't have perceived that that was a stretch or an uptake in responsibilities, but at the new company HR was much more highly respected and they didn't only think of her as a capital markets sales person. She has gone on, in the last 8 or 9 years, to be one of the most senior HR managers globally. And she knew absolutely nothing about HR until her early forties. But she obviously knew people really well. She knew the content of the business really well and the bank she's at was confident it could teach her about HR. It was able to leverage her prior experience, which obviously gave her a huge amount of credibility. I don't know nearly as many success stories as I think there should exist with women. I know lots of success stories like that with men.'

This is an important perspective to consider: women are often not given the same flexible career 'journeys' as men. Whether it is an issue of male executives (wrongly) assuming that women are risk-averse or even not qualified to perform career-intensive roles, it has been empirically demonstrated that women are more often overlooked for such roles, and pigeon-holed, than their male counterparts.[xxxi]

Google, in its relatively short lifespan has succeeded in becoming the World's Best Company to Work For [xxxii] and that is no accident. Enabling working structures that encourage employees to think for themselves in areas important to them will lead to unexpected results. Google, interestingly, does not lose as much female talent as other corporations.

Box 2: Google Case Study

According to Sarah Speake, Industry Director for Technology at Google, there are three key areas which make a difference for Google's female employees leading to lower attrition levels in the industry.

1. Focus on employee well-being:
The Google founders 'maintain a culture where it is more important to have the fringe benefits so that people feel that

the organisation is maintaining its promise to them. We have an ergonomics expert who visits anybody, particularly early on returning from maternity leave, or anybody with posture, neck or back problems, so that they can advise them about the working environment; we have a huge team of people dedicated to the well-being of our staff which has enabled us to create this amazing, highly collaborative environment. The open nature of our unique culture also forms the basis of our product launches, the cornerstone of our mission to make the world's information globally accessible and useful.'

2. Unorthodox recruitment:
'My story of being recruited and then promoted when I was on maternity leave is pretty unique. Not many organisations would even embark on that journey. I was an unknown quantity. They did not know me well enough to be absolutely sure that when I said during the first interview process, literally a week before I gave birth, that I was definitely capable of coming back after six months' maternity leave, potentially longer. But equally there are men in our organisation that set a very good example. I report directly to Matt Brittin, our UK and Ireland Managing Director, and he makes time to be with his family. He alters his working week to accommodate his children's activities. That's important, and I think that unless any organisation has that behaviour at senior role model level — only then can it be part of the culture.'

3. Google '20% Time':
'20 percent time' was originally founded in our engineering community; the idea being that 20% of any engineer's time should be dedicated to creating innovative new products and tools. They can work on creating something new and, any project that comes out of it which the Board approves as a viable business proposition, is then given additional Engineering resource – in fact, that's how Gmail was launched. The equivalent approach in non-Engineering divisions such as my

own allows me to drive Google's involvement in critical external initiatives such as Connecting Women in Technology; Women in Technology and inter-company mentoring for example. As long as we get our day jobs done, of course! We also use a lot of our own cloud-based collaboration tools to share ideas and best practice, which continues to create a highly collaborative, innovative culture that I'm personally very proud to be a part of.

Understand that stereotyping still happens and why it happens

Our own research is backed up by Catalyst research, which consistently highlights that negative stereotyping is one of the biggest barriers for the progression of women in the corporate world[xxxiii]. This stereotyping takes the form of assumptions made on the perceived (reduced) capabilities after starting a family discussed above. Women are not offered challenging roles nor international assignments in the belief that they will not take them. As one our survey respondents said, 'Appreciate that maternity is not the end of the world, offer women the same opportunities to grow as men.'

It is important to appreciate the relative, average differences between the genders, but always to ensure that exceptions are considered. We don't all fall into 'typical' categories. For instance, it is increasingly the case that men look for shared parenting roles, and they too face the stigma attached to flexible working. According to the Fatherhood Institute in London, one in four families is experiencing 'dad gap'. A recent poll of 1,000 parents highlighted that 'an overwhelming majority of mothers and fathers want to share changing nappies, reading with their kids and taking their children to doctor and dentist appointments, with significant numbers wanting longer, better paid paternity leave and more flexible working dads'[xxxiv].

So why does stereotyping happen? The short answer is shortcuts. Our brain consists of over 180 billion neurons, each processing information through 15,000 synapses per second. So, to be efficient and save energy, the brain 'cheats' and creates shortcuts for processing information. 'For example, although you move your head and eyes constantly, your brain does not lose track of the objects surrounding you. So that it is not overwhelmed with information processing, the brain makes predictions about what it is seeing and changes its predictions only when it makes an error.' *Gregory Berns*[xxxv]. This neural 'cheating', also called Predictive Coding (when our brain 'fills the gaps'), is what leads us to make quick assumptions about others, and is the basis of stereotyping. In order to make change, our brain requires a break from past experiences, and to be forced to think in a different way. This is where the crux lies in overcoming barriers to gender-stereotyping in business.

Overcoming gender-stereotyping requires change. We need to encourage organisation-wide neurogenesis, the creation of new synaptic connections through experience.

Breaking Stereotypes through organisational change

Implementing diversity strategies of any type, be it of gender, culture, age or disability, means that the cultural fabric of an organisation needs to be adapted. As with any radical social transition, the most challenging aspect is managing the people and their resistance to change.

We can learn from nature about how to overcome our prejudices. The way our bodies mend following injury offers a blueprint for implementing diversity strategies to create inclusive business cultures. Let's assume that an organisation has a sporting injury which has been caused by poor technique.

Phase 1: Accept and understand the Injury

Look at the organisation. Analyse the numbers: how many women are there at each level? Is there a level at which women are absent? Have previous diversity initiatives worked? If the organisation structure looks similar to the diagram below, the answer is no. The organisation is sustaining repeated heavy injuries on the female side due to poor technique in the culture. Accept that change is needed.

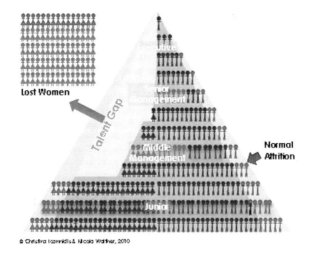

© Christina Ioannidis & Nicola Walther, 2010

Diagram 4: The Abnormal Attrition Triangle

The first step of this process is to understand why prejudice and bias is normal and present in everyone. Humans have muscle memory and for every activity we repeatedly perform, our muscles adapt to give us optimal performance. Muscles develop according to need so a marathon runner, for example, develops differently from, say, a swimmer and, if an athlete has an injury caused by incorrect technique, a different support structure would be built by the body, exercising and developing muscle groups in different ways. This is entirely possible with hard, consistent work. The same is true for organisations. In order to redress bias, it is important to understand that a preferred way of doing things exists in everyone and every organisation and we must understand that the process of change will be tough, but that it is possible.

Leading psychologist Binna Kandola talks about facing biases head-on, in a three-step process:

1. Understand biases exist in all of us (Phase 1)

2. Become aware of our own biases (Phase 2)

3. Break the connection between bias and action (Phase 3)[xxxvi]

Phase 2: Gauging the Muscular Shortfall (or pain)

As with a sporting injury, measurement and awareness of the problem is essential when developing a treatment plan. One company, PricewaterhouseCoopers, collected data from performance management evaluations of its staff. It compared the progress of the highest performing men and women. The company discovered that the progression rates for women rated as high-performing were slower than for their male counterparts. To educate the business on this disparity, it developed a forecast system (called Flowrates) based on its own actuaries' readings of the pattern of development to be expected of those high performers.

Organisations need to identify where the weaknesses lie. Is there a structural issue, or are there areas where bias may be preventing minority groups from being assimilated into the business? Are there pockets of the business where women are 'locked out'? How is that likely to be affecting the business negatively; in terms of disengagement, loss to top talent, discrimination suits? And how can the muscle fabric in those parts of the organisation be rearranged and rebuilt?

At PricewaterhouseCoopers, the organisation identified the ranks of the business where women seemed to 'leak out', at Managing Partner, Non-Equity Partner and Partner level. The organisation set up the Gender Advisory Council which performed in-depth research on:

> Why women were not progressing at those levels
>
> Establishing accountabilities for redressing that lack of progress and
>
> Developing an effective planning process, increasing personal awareness on the cultural and human elements of the problem.[xxxvii]

Phase 3: Working Through the Pain

One-off training is not viable when making long-term changes to your technique in a sporting environment. Breaking old habits takes a significant effort over the long term. Similarly, to overcome organisational and structural bias, it is likely that a culture change is needed. Breaking set behaviour-patterns requires long-term investment because the brain needs to be reprogrammed.

According to the neuroscientist Gregory Berns, 'Sometimes a simple change of environment is enough to jog the perceptual system out of familiar categories. When confronted with places never seen before, the brain must create new categories. It is in this process that the brain jumbles around old ideas with new images to create new syntheses.' [xxxviii]

It is this consistent bombarding of our brain with new stimuli that leads to cultural change. In the same way, those who have experienced physical injury know that rehabilitation requires mental as well as localised physical intervention. Our brain has consciously to send signals to the ailing part of the body to 'wake' the areas momentarily disengaged in the recuperation process. The same is true for organisations.

Once the shortcomings have been identified and there is a clear rationale about why new diversity activities should be introduced, it is important to look bias in the eye. A good tool for assessing and tackling bias is the Implicit Association Test (IAT). The IAT allows the measurement of associations that can reliably reveal unconscious biases in individuals. Painful as it may be to face personal bias, tests have shown that training people on these tests has significantly improved thinking.

For example, a team member may believe that they do not have a bias against women in business; however, when shown images of women and men and asked to record a response for each gender in the context of business, it will often be seen that there is a minor positive bias for men and against women in business. These biases affect the perception of women and, hence, behavioural responses to them in the context of business, and vice versa.

Following the IAT, it is important to clarify where, when and how we will behave in a particular way. As Kandola puts it, 'It is a way of directing our attention to particular contexts in which we are likely to act from unconscious habit rather than conscious intention. We train ourselves to recognise situations in which we want to act differently.'[xxxix]

To redress the imbalance of gender-based stereotyping of women as business leaders, one of the most powerful ways is to use the IAT is to present positive images of women as leaders. Much in the same way as physiotherapy requires us to work through pain to rebuild muscle fibre, this unconsciously reconditions the brain to attach positive imagery with the out-group, in this case the women, and thus reverses the traditional prejudices held by the in-group, men.

This is positive, simple, cost-effective and a 'show' rather than a 'tell' exercise. It retrains the brain by triggering mental associations in a direct manner.

Building on the individual-bias reversal process, it is important to expand gender-stereotyping reversal activities throughout the organisation. Because organisations are made up of individuals, reaffirming the group's commitment to remove gender-bias is required as part of group-bias reversal activities.

The activities for long-term reversal of systemic bias include:

> Implementing a strategy of breaking gender stereotypes in internal and external communications: promote women and men in 'non'-traditional fields, using case studies, images and success stories so that gender associations are removed from job titles and responsibilities

> Coaching and training employees on the different cultural backgrounds and different styles of working between women and men. Here too, supporting these visible exceptions to the rule is critical so that the natural tendency to pigeon-hole is avoided.

> Developing an inclusive culture: foster a culture of inclusion with the help of a gender-neutral development tool which break down the barriers between the out- and the in-group (women and men, respectively). Point out the similarities between individuals in the groups, even if they may seem different. Building familiarity through communication is critical in removing barriers of prejudice.

Phase 4: Building Muscle Strength and Bulk

As a recovering athlete does, it is necessary for organisations to build on their internal culture's inclusive muscle strength so that new techniques may become ingrained in the culture. The main activities in this extensive phase include:

> Providing leadership coaching, fighting bias head-on. Individuals who patronise others should be confronted with their bias. By the same token, victims of this abuse should learn to appeal to the 'perpetrator's' sense of fairness by openly questioning them.

> Creating and implementing perspective-taking frameworks. It is critical for women to work with male and female mentors in a challenging business context and use the learning experience to gain perspectives in gender sensitivity and business acumen and skills development. As seen in Chapter 2, more than traditional training, these learning activities need to revolve around business activities and should be supported by individual coaching programmes to recognise how the coachee's perceptions may change and how they may now act differently in view of their own initial prejudices.

This phase is about implementing meritocratic recruitment and promotion processes:

> **Hire on merit:** Hire non-traditional candidates through skills-based assessments and by asking, 'How can this person do this job?'[xl]

> **Collective and Reverse Hiring:** Include subordinates in the selection process for their line managers, different panels for the selection of individuals to a team. Break the traditional

hiring mould by engaging in a collective hiring process with mixed groups of individuals from different backgrounds to interview prospective candidates. We support Ricardo Semler's views that this is 'a time-honoured thousand-year-old method of admitting members to the tribe. Cavemen and fellows in medieval artisan guilds worked no differently. They are all based on a decision on how well a group accepts a newcomer' [xli].

Blind hiring: Conduct interview rounds with a non-traditional talent pool where opportunities for bias are removed, such as virtual interviews with potential employees where names, personal details and indicators to ethnicity are removed. Focus on the individual skill-set rather than the physical attributes.

Performance evaluation: Conduct 360° assessments on how an employee has demonstrated they can perform their role. Ask what are their personal strengths. What do they want to do? What do they enjoy doing? Where would they naturally fit in into the organisation's requirements? We frequently find individuals in roles unsuited to their skills and interests. Fitting candidates in where both they and the organisation want them to be promotes autonomy and encourages the talent to define how it works. As Chapter 2 highlighted, this is a core requirement for entrepreneurial women who were previously corporate talent. As one of our respondents, a former investment banker commented, 'Now I can spend my time on what I most care about. I set my own standard and decide not just what I'm going to be doing but how I'm going to do it. I find that very motivating.'

Succession planning: Identify how a person who does not come from the 'traditional' talent pool can suit a particular senior role. Provide shadowing opportunities to see how they may feel about 'stepping up' to a new role or function and the support systems they require. 'I've seen some companies, but not a lot, have what I would call an internal headhunter. So today I think it's far too easy for an employee to take a call externally from a headhunter and move rather than look at opportunities internally and say, actually I'm currently stalled or plateaued where I am. So I think the best companies really do proactively manage their human capital and this role of the internal headhunter helps to make sure that the talent and leadership capabilities are continually stretched and pushed and leveraged.' *Kate Grussing*

Talent Management: Engage the individual and review their career life-stages and motivations throughout them. Ensure that their work is clearly satisfying their individual passions, as outlined in Chapter 2.

Phase 5: Constant Muscle Growth: Review and Reassessment

Like the athlete who needs to maintain top physical performance in the newly reformed muscles, organisations need consistently to build and review the on-going progress of the organisation's diversity development. Success of these activities, in terms of individual bias-reduction, individual engagement, succession planning, gender-specific employee turnover, has to be monitored and compared in the long term.

The key ways to monitor success are:

> Measure progress
> Compare long-term metrics
> Review and investigate shortfalls

It is only by long-term therapy that a person recovers from injury – in the same way that redressing stereotyping and relaxing the current muscle structure of an organisation requires a long-term approach and a concerted investment to create a sustainable, gender-neutral business environment for the benefit of all the internal and external stakeholders.

Conclusion

This chapter has highlighted the need for organisations to embrace the differences in the way values and beliefs manifest themselves. From an individual and organisational perspective, it is critical to establish processes to remind and prevent us from letting our brains cheat, become lazy and entrench negative stereotyping.

Breaking gender stereotypes also implies changing the traditional roles of men in society. If there is something that this recent recession has brought about it is increasing role-reversal: coined as a 'mancession'. The credit crunch has produced more women breadwinners, and the tradition of men as breadwinners of the family unit has been turned on its head[xlii]. Men have increasingly taken on the full-time parenting roles, which has prepared the way for a complete societal and stereotype-breaking shift.

The focus should be on offering experience within business to break stereotypes, particularly to educate *both* genders. However, it is uncomfortable to have to remind ourselves of our blind-spots and that we need to find ways to see around them. Neurogenesis, the creation of fresh paths in unfamiliar individual or organisational mental territory, is not easy. It requires commitment from the business and tolerance for doing things in new ways.

Chapter 4: Collaboration

'Education consists mainly in what we have unlearned'
Mark Twain

Learning to collaborate with people who think
differently is hard work. Successful collaboration
requires education because it means learning to accept
differences, even when it is instinctive to value
similarities and to strive to fit in. We are programmed
from birth to fit in with the tribe so as not to be alone
and in danger. A small child mimics constantly,
learning to fit in by copying what his elders do.

Our need for similarity is understandable but the key in
business is to recognise this tendency and learn to
mitigate the effect of exclusion in the workplace.
People with different perspectives bring with them a
range of experiences. It may be necessary to unlearn
habits formed from our own experience to accept their
contribution. Through understanding and a culture of
accepting difference, it is possible to integrate people

with different perspectives without requiring adherence to one way of thinking.

In this chapter we will show how an organisation can adopt a new, more collaborative culture using existing resources. We explain why a collaborative culture builds stronger organisations, and how it is the third and crucial part of achieving and valuing gender balance.

What does a collaborative culture achieve?

Increased Collaboration

Increased Innovation

Retention of Women and Improved Profits

Of the women we surveyed, 48% stated that 'a chance to be more creative' was one thing which welcomed them into their new entrepreneurial lives. Creativity ranked joint first alongside 'more control and flexibility over my life'. This dual desire was unexpected even to us, but exposes a clear reason for women to leave corporate life. They feel creatively stifled. A collaborative culture leads to greater creativity through innovation and will therefore help retain high-performing women.

We have already given some data about the improved financial performance of organisations with more women in senior roles in Chapter 1. McKinsey and Co's *Women Matter* report goes further, emphasising that not only do companies with a higher proportion of women in their top management have better financial performance[xliii], but

> 'Companies with three or more women in top management functions score more highly for each organisational performance criterion than companies with no women at the top…'

This is supported further by a recent study undertaken by the prestigious Michigan Institute of Technology's Centre for Collective Intelligence and Carnegie Mellon. The study concluded that the number of women in a team or group makes a difference to its effectiveness in solving difficult problems. The researchers came to their conclusions based on 'the higher social sensibility exhibited by females, on average'.[xliv] It is thus not difficult to see why women's natural propensity as integrators of ideas makes them an integral catalyst to improving a group, or even a corporate board's collective intelligence.

Innovation and gender balance

According to the London Centre for Women in Business, '[On a team level…] the key levers and drivers for innovative processes are positively influenced by having 50:50 proportions of men and women… This clearly shows that equal gender representation can help to unlock the innovative potential of teams'[xlv]

These findings demonstrate compatibility between the genders in fuelling innovation. To encourage innovation, it is necessary to avoid 'group-think' and peel away all mental blind-spots. Creating gender-balanced teams is a way to achieve this. Gender-balanced and ethnically diverse teams are thus critical in the modern workplace. Different value-systems, mental preferences and individual identities construct the powerhouse of innovation.

Sarah Gibbs, a former Ernst & Young employee in New Zealand and the founder of Trilogy cosmetics, explained, 'I've got a very flexible approach to marketing at Trilogy. I say to everyone that anyone can have a great idea and if you're not in marketing and you have a great initiative then you are going to feel great about yourself. Three years ago our accountant came up with a sensational marketing concept which we have executed every year since then. He's still here and every year he gets praised for his sensational initiative. He's a guy where we're predominantly girls...'. The accountant broke through the walls of his profession to propose a completely new idea, which was a huge success. The open and accepting environment allowed him to achieve this.

Innovation and bringing your whole self to work

Modern psychologists are exercised by the importance of Identity Integration: the drawing on different areas of knowledge for increased creativity. This permits the expression of the whole self in an open, safe and non-stereotyped culture. For example, creating an environment in which a woman can be an engineer and a woman at work, rather than having to behave like a man just because she's operating in a male-dominated profession, can have great results.

'People with higher levels of Identity Integration display higher levels of creativity when problems require that they draw on their different realms of knowledge[xlvi]'; the researchers found 'that women engineering students with high Identity Integration ('perceiving their gender and professional identities to be compatible') were more innovative when they were asked to design a cell phone for women… It appears that for tasks that require drawing on knowledge systems related to both their gender and professional identities, women with high Identity Integration were more able to bring these knowledge systems to the task simultaneously, resulting in higher levels of innovation.'[xlvii]

This can work the other way around. One of our high-flying interviewees who left a large financial institution described low levels of Identity Integration. She explained that she felt as if she were on a theatre stage when she went to work. She needed to be somebody else in order to conform. Not being allowed to be herself at work manifested itself as stress and, ultimately, she left.

Innovation and creating the right working environment

As the examples above, of the accountant and the telephone designers, show, allowing people to be themselves in a non-judgmental, balanced environment leads to improved innovation and creativity for both these reasons.

One of our survey respondents said, 'Don't limit creativity in politics.' Organisations should be encouraged to employ a democratic approach to problem-solving. Allow people to be themselves, whatever their affinity group, and the innovative talent latent in the organisation will be released. Women have a natural capacity for integrating their identities with their working practices, irrespective of industry or company. This ability flourishes when the environment allows for creative tension without political overtones.

One of our interviewees gave us a couple of graphic analogies on organisational politics and innovation, 'The way that my organisation protects innovation is to put projects under the sponsorship of very senior managers in the company. This way the project can't be attacked by the rest of the organisation. Innovation by its nature behaves like a virus in the organisation because it's different. As you dive in with a new innovation, the company antibodies try to kill the virus, and you've got to protect it until it has enough structure to live on its own.

The other mistake corporations make is "pulling the plant up and looking at the roots all the time". The company pulls a plant up and says, "Are you growing?" If the company is forever doing this, the governance of the main body of the organisation weighs heavily on the innovation. If you're not strong enough (a) to say it doesn't apply or (b) get some process people around you (e.g., a very good programme manager who deals with all of the reporting issues that could slow a project down) you're forever being asked, "Are you there yet?", "Are you big enough yet?", "Have you got enough revenue?"

Also, in a large organisation such as ours (with net sales of over \$40bn), early stage innovative projects are not even a rounding error. A million here or a million there is nothing as a revenue. Sponsorship from senior management therefore allows for the right amount of attention without the governance of the whole organisation weighing too heavily on the project.'

Use existing resources to stimulate collaboration

Use the networks for business

Many businesses approach the issue of diversity through internal networks. The creation of women's networks and other affinity groups gives short-term momentum and a general sense of positive change because women feel more supported.

Despite the best of intentions, these affinity groups can run out of steam if they have no real purpose within the business. Networks must contribute to the delivery of the organisation's commercial vision. If they do not deliver real business output they segregate the group from the business. This can be damaging to the aim of increasing female representation in leadership positions. The result is that mentoring circles become stale and solid.

What is needed to generate real value from the networks in an organisation?

1. Align the Network with corporate strategy

Align the network's objectives with the organisation's vision and strategy. If the aim is to become the world's premier consulting group in a particular segment, the network should be accountable and contribute to that mission.

2. Create working groups to address particular business issues

Utilise the power of the women's network in creating work-groups to solve problems and generate new ideas and approaches to developing the business. Human Resources and Talent Management are an obvious area where targeted work-groups can deliver measurable results. As we shall see in Chapters 6 and 7, this should be extended to the other parts of the business.

3. Invest in networks as you would in a new business venture

When sponsoring network activities, approach them as a venture capitalist investing in an entrepreneurial project would. Ensure the returns are communicated tangibly. Even 'soft' concepts such as engagement can be measured using simple metrics. Set business expectations: X investment = Y returns. The networks will then run their activities as a business, with measurable results and become, in the long term, beneficial case-studies of success.

4. Invest in Dedicated Resource

Networks are frequently run by professionals who also have a 'day job'. This is counter-productive and indicates that diversity management is not being aligned with business strategy. A dedicated resource to design and implement such a wide-ranging initiative is needed.

This will seem a hard-nosed approach to managing diversity. However, it is critical for any business to take this approach if it is to make long-lasting, cost-effective and beneficial change.

Innovate by allowing for new experience and partnerships

The overwhelming majority of women entrepreneurs in our survey claimed that learning gained in one industry and applied to another is critical for success in business. Over 85% of our respondents said that corporations should appreciate this capacity.

In his book *Iconoclast*, neuroscientist Gregory Berns analyses the behaviours of the likes of Steve Jobs and Martin Luther King, Jr. and explains why they were and are able to challenge the status quo. He emphasises that radical new experiences have most impact when attempting to change the way people think. 'The neural networks in our brain that govern both perception and imagination can be reprogrammed … But it is difficult to do this in business-as-usual conditions. It typically takes a novel stimulus … The more radical and novel the change, the greater the likelihood of new insights being generated.' [xlviii].

New mothers certainly have radical new experiences but we are not suggesting childbirth is the only way to open the minds of employees! Forming partnerships outside the immediate social and professional sphere, working on projects with multiple inputs, and learning to work with new people will build stronger teams with greater powers of innovation.

We encourage organisations to develop every opportunity for employees to collaborate on free-thinking projects with stakeholders (e.g., customers, as above). What we call Transformational Partnerships will occur when the simple question, 'How we can work together for mutual benefit?' is answered. We have developed the CLIC's Framework as a blueprint for creating Transformational Partnerships with customers (and other stakeholders).

Each of the steps in the process is identified in the diagram overleaf.

CONNECT
Extend relationships, understand spheres of influence,
engage in powerful rapport strategies

LEARN
Understand motivators and how they work; gauge desires.
Discover what impresses the stakeholder groups from what
they say and do

INSPIRE
Build additional value by solving problems that may have
originally fallen outside the scope of work of the project

CREATE
Develop targeted proposals to meet needs; design strategies
to encourage movement beyond the original scope on a win-
win basis. What can we do better together?

SHARE
Work together on dedicated implementation. Develop intra-
organisational relationships for effective communication and
enhanced ongoing productivity

Diagram 5: CLICs Framework for Transformational
Partnerships

Be realistic about failure as an inevitable by-product of innovation

Frans Johansson, author of *The Medici Effect* states that 'in any given field of creative activity, it is typical to find that around 10% of creators are responsible for 50% of all contributions'[xlix]. His research identified that innovative people 'experience more failures than their less creative counterparts because they pursue more ideas' and that in true innovation 'planning for failure' is a necessary and unavoidable element.

This resonated with the ex-corporate women in our research who were clear that 'failures are potential'. As entrepreneurs they say that dealing with failure is critical. They also had this mind-set as corporate employees. This implies that, for them, failure forms part of a course of innovation, or experimentation. Women spoke loud and clear – failure is there to be learned from.

Box 3: Rite-Solutions Case Study

US software company, Rite-Solutions, boasts a 2% attrition rate (normally at 10-20% in the industry). It attracted attention through its novel approach towards encouraging innovation. All employees are awarded a $10,000 pot of 'opinion money' at the start of their employment. This can be invested in ideas in the company's internal idea stock market, which is called Mutual Fun. Each stock comes with a detailed description called an Expect-Us and begins trading at a price of $10. Employees signal their enthusiasm by investing in a stock and, better yet, volunteering to work on the project. To generate revenue, employees have to put in time working on an idea, moving it from concept to reality. Volunteers share in the proceeds, in the form of real money, if the stock becomes a product or delivers savings. Mr Marino, president and co-founder of Rite-Solutions, says the market, which began in January 2005, has already paid big dividends. One of the earliest stocks (ticker symbol: VIEW) was a proposal to apply three-dimensional visualisation technology, akin to video games, to help sailors and domestic-security personnel practise making decisions in emergency situations. Initially, Mr Marino was unenthusiastic about the idea — 'I'm not a joystick jockey' — but support among employees was overwhelming. By March 2006, the product line, called Rite-View, accounted for 30% of total sales.

Mr Lavoie, the other co-founder, added that another virtue of the stock market is that it finds good ideas from unlikely sources. Among Rite-Solutions' core technologies are pattern-recognition algorithms used in military applications, as well as for electronic gambling systems at casinos, a big market for the company. A member of the administrative staff, with no technical expertise, thought that this technology might also be used in educational settings, to create an entertaining way for students to learn history or mathematics.

She started a stock called Win/Play/Learn (symbol: WPL), which attracted a rush of investment from engineers eager to turn her idea into a product. Their enthusiasm led to meetings with Hasbro, and Rite-Solutions won a contract to help it build its VuGo multimedia system.

Rite-Solutions created a true incubator for ideas that, more importantly, allows individuals to create their own jobs.

Recognise and appreciate innovation

Recognition is extremely important for women. One of our survey respondents recommends to employers who want to retain women, 'Give due credit and gratitude to women's contribution. Ensure that you listen to them and consider that their input is going to be distinctive, even if unexpected.' The perception that their contribution was not being recognised was the third highest percentage factor for women in our survey leaving their employer, with 27% saying this was one of the reasons they left.

Unfortunately, one of the main instruments for recognition within organisations is remuneration, which is a blunt, impersonal instrument. Paying someone more doesn't necessarily improve their creativity. In fact, research on rewarding creativity has uncovered that 'external expectations and rewards can kill the intrinsic motivation and thus kill creativity'[li].

Fair and transparent pay is important because it is a form of recognition and speaks to women's other values as discussed in Chapter 1, but when it comes to innovation, organisations need to be more creative and more personal. We suggest that even personal thanks and appreciation from a senior manager who has seen the output of a project will go a long way towards motivating a female employee. Use imagination to recognise and reward the innovators' imaginations.

Conclusion

This chapter has highlighted the connections between
gender diversity and innovation. It has set the case for
forging ways to overcome traditional ways of doing
things to create inclusive, collaborative cultures.
Google and Rite-Solutions present examples of
entrepreneurially minded corporate cultures, which
create value by leveraging the innovative capabilities of
their employees. These companies have developed
corporate cultures that have shown lower-than-average
employee attrition rates. Respondents to our survey
and interviews firmly believed that what these
companies have achieved is possible within the context
of larger corporates. What is needed, however, is an
unwavering corporate-wide commitment from the top
and the grassroots of the organisation to create a
sustainable Gender-Savvy culture.

Chapter 5: Sustainability

Sustainability is the capacity to endure. The Earth Charter speaks of 'a sustainable global society founded on respect for nature, universal human rights, economic justice, and a culture of peace.'

In this chapter we will look at the role sustainability plays in women's outlook. Women are natural nurturers. Women are at the heart of the environmental and social revolution. Women we spoke to strive to be at the centre of their world, their community, and feel a responsibility to keep a watchful eye over future generations.

Why is sustainability important in retention of women and business development?

In today's demanding, highly competitive working environment, talent sustainability strategies are not only important for retaining female talent, but critical for attracting future generations, starting from Generation

Y. Female consumers (representing the majority of consumers today) are more likely to make purchasing decisions based on the attractiveness of a cause or in support of social and environmental improvement.

Women's exodus driven by values (not value)

Our research has highlighted that 31% of women who left the corporate sphere thought that their 'values did not align with the company's'. This is supported by the Work-Life Policy Research On Ramps/Off Ramps report, where women's motivators at work include 'deriving meaning and purpose' and 'giving back to society'. These overshadowed any financial rewards or the value of their pay cheque, which were the main motivators for men.

Men will compartmentalise with greater ease, women are synthesisers of ideas, actions and lives. As such, the company's soul, its social consciousness is deeply engrained in her needs, and in order to retain her loyalty, any organisation needs to take this into consideration. This is the intersection between a woman's multiple roles as professional, family organiser and social nurturer.

An organisation's sustainability credentials drive purchasing decisions and brand value

Cone, a US-based strategic communications firm specialising in Cause Branding, conducted an online survey[lii] which describes a marketplace where mothers (Moms) and Generation Y (Millennials) are the two most sought-after consumer marketing segments.

These groups are more sensitised than the overall population to the role a corporation plays in supporting or destroying the community, and the world. This has a strong impact on the brand equity of the products they consume. The same is true for the employer brand – for both existing or future employers.

Box 4: Women, Generation Y and Sustainability

MOMS AND MILLENNIALS – IN THE MARKETPLACE

Moms and Millennials are the two most sought-after consumer marketing segments for a reason. Moms control about 80 percent of the household shopping,[1] and college-aged Millennials have near $40 billion in discretionary income to spend.[2] Still, each wants to shop wisely, and more than any other demographic groups we tested, they buy with an eye toward the greater good.

Millennials[3]
Ninety-four percent of respondents ages 18-24 find it acceptable for a company to involve a cause or issue in its marketing (vs 88% average). As the chart indicates, these Millennials are only slightly more likely to switch brands, but they are much more willing to try new products because of a cause affiliation. They are also particularly attuned to causes outside of their shopping decisions as they seek opportunities to become more deeply engaged and advocate on behalf of important issues. And more than any other cohort, cause plays a significant role in where this age segment chooses to work. A company's commitment to a cause helps drive their decisions in and out of the store. Millennials' passion for supporting causes presents significant growth opportunities for companies as these young adults' income and purchasing power grows.

Moms[4]

For all the attention given to Millennials and youth today, moms really are the epitome of the cause consumer. Perhaps because they control the purse-strings and have socially minded youth influencing their buying decisions behind the scenes, they are open to being marketed to when it comes to cause brands, and they are virtually unanimous in shopping with a cause in mind:

95% find cause marketing acceptable (vs 88% average);
93% are likely to switch brands (vs 80% average); and,
92% want to buy a product that supports a cause (vs 81% average).

The numbers speak for themselves, and their message is quite clear: When it comes to cause branding, Millennials and Moms matter most.

[1] eMarketer. "'How Retailers Can Reach Moms.'" February 23, 2010. http://www.emarketer.com/Article.aspx?R=1007529
[2] MediaPost. "'Returning College Students Spending Optimistically.'" July 19, 2010. http://www.mediapost.com/publications/?fa=Articles.showArticle&art_aid=13 2165
[3] "'Millennials'" refers to survey respondents 18-24 years old. This is only one age segment of the entire Millennial generation.
[4] "'Moms'" refers to female survey respondents who have children of 17 or under living in their household.

Shopping attitudes and behaviors:	Total	Millennials	Moms
Believe cause marketing is acceptable	88%	94%	95%
Bought a cause product/service in past 12 months	41%	53%	61%
Likely to switch brands	80%	85%	93%
Willing to try a NEW brand or one they've never heard of	61%	73%	73%
Willing to buy a more expensive brand	19%	26%	27%

Cause branding is important when they decide:	Total	Millennials	Moms
Which companies they want to see doing business in their communities	79%	88%	90%
Which products and services to recommend to other people	76%	86%	88%
What to buy or where to shop	75%	84%	88%
Where to work	69%	87%	79%
Which stocks or mutual funds to invest in	59%	79%	74%

They want opportunities to support causes, such as:	Total	Millennials	Moms
Buy a product in which a portion of the sales goes to the support of the cause or issue	81%	85%	92%
Learn about a social or environmental issue	80%	86%	91%
Make changes to their own behavior, such as get more physical activity, eat healthier or reduce their impact on the environment	78%	84%	88%
Offer their ideas and feedback on the company's cause-related efforts and programs	75%	83%	89%
Donate money to a nonprofit the company has identified	75%	84%	88%
Serve as an advocate for an issue they care about, such as signing a petition or engaging their community	72%	82%	81%
Volunteer for the cause or issue	72%	81%	85%

Reproduced with the kind permission of Cone[liii]

How does that soul, that humane face in a company support women within an organisation? How does that translate into the process by which those who leave the business are managed? How are they reached, and engaged in honest dialogue on what they value and where the organisation can make a difference to their life?

Focus on Sustainable Talent Management

Successful employers in managing gender diversity are also those brands which implement processes to engage continuously with their employees and customers in sustainable service. They integrate the product and the world of their consumer seamlessly.

McDonalds' introduction of play areas and Ronald McDonald to entertain the children, or Starbuck's free 'babyccino' (frothy milk) for the baby as mothers enjoy their morning coffee, are examples of brands enabling women to bring their extended world into their brand experience. The same ideal is true for the workplace. Companies need to demonstrate authentic care for female employees and their extended world or circle of influence (or dependants).

1. Fulfil Her at Work: The key areas for this have been covered in the previous chapters:

> Walk the talk: ask for, listen and act on her needs; focus on her passions and appreciate her individual strengths.

Develop supporting structures to produce flexibility in both working and work-type – the concept of non-traditional, sustainable, working arrangements.

Build Mentoring Meshes to extend her circle of influence within and outside the business, as well as to increase her personal development opportunities. One of our survey respondents summarised this beautifully. When asked what companies need to do to harness female talent, she said they should offer 'training, recognition, authority, responsibility, and access to mentors'.

Foster true democracy: discourage hierarchy in the organisation. Instill open and team-based recruitment processes, establish transparent succession-planning, based on merit and diversity of experience and relevant skills.

2. Embrace Her World: as mentioned in Chapter 1, women are challenged when their home, work and family responsibilities collide. It is important to understand that in a woman's world a company needs to recognise that close family and dependants are not separate but an extension of her being.

One of our survey respondents emphasised, 'Understand that no matter how much we love our work, we also have family lives'. The opportunities for organisations to develop this concept are endless.

Introduce services: provide services that remove the stress of performing small yet time-consuming tasks for dual-career couples. For example:

> Introduce personal concierge services
>
> Offer virtual personal assistants
>
> Offer on-site crèches or emergency nanny schemes.

Organisations have introduced concierge or childcare services but often without properly consulting the workforce. Employees should be asked what they really want and need rather than spending money on something which is little more than going through the motions for appearance's sake. What looks good in a company brochure may have little practical value.

Here is an example. Jane's nanny was sick on a day when both she and her husband had critical meetings. Jane had to leave her one-year-old, who had never been left alone outside home before, at the emergency crèche. He screamed so much that he made himself sick and after 90 minutes the crèche had to ask her to collect him. A more sympathetic and imaginative scheme was introduced by other companies, whereby children usually looked after at home were sent an emergency nanny.

Adapt your mind-set: this question should be answered, 'What else can be done to make her life easier, simpler, better?' Assume the role of catalyst to her optimal performance, not just her employer.

One of our coachees, a legal counsel for a leading investment consulting firm, was feeling uninspired by her organisation and her role. Working with her we uncovered that her sense of personal fulfilment would be enhanced if she could embrace, and somehow involve, a charity which meant a lot to her personally. She decided to set up multiple sponsorship and fund-raising opportunities through her employer and now her employer is developing a collaborative product of which the charity will be a beneficiary.

These inclusive and considerate activities should not be limited to the employee only. Look for opportunities to involve her friends, extended family, and the causes she cares for; encourage sustainable investments and involvement of her external world for the benefit of the community, the business, and, most importantly, herself. Invite her circle of close contacts to days out volunteering or performing community support work. Invite partners to the year-end parties. These are opportunities to build authentic relationships with them too. Engage with them as stakeholders of an asset in which the organisation is investing.

Do this consistently, rather than just once a year. We know companies have introduced the 'daughters to work' days, where parents can bring their daughters to work, but nothing more. These daughters are not only future consumers of products, they are, more importantly, the future talent of organisations. So, how can the organisation engage with this group in a meaningful way? How can the organisation learn from what they have to say about the company and brand?

Box 5: Macdonalds Case Study

McDonalds is an excellent example of the above. The company celebrates 'McFamily' – evident both in its retail environment and services through to employees' strong commitment to one another. This was demonstrated by how quickly the employers mobilised to respond to Hurricane Katrina in the US and the earthquake in China. Each McDonald's franchisee is encouraged by the franchise structure, to build strong ties between its restaurant managers and the communities in which they have their business.

Sustain relationships with Stakeholders (including leavers)

Women, and increasingly men, are living lives full of changes and scenic career routes. The one-track career, as discussed in Chapter 3, is of limited reality to talent today, particularly women. Women do not want to be derailed from their careers, but an unappealing environment and negative stereotyping pushes them out. While women do 'off-ramp', they often do not want to sever all contact with their former employers.

At the key point of intersection in their mid 30s when family responsibility beckons, women are plagued by a tremendous sense of guilt in turning their backs on their careers. This is further exacerbated by line managers who assume that because a woman is taking a side-step in her career, she will not want to continue working at all. Our research has proved that this is not the case. Women want a sustainable transition.

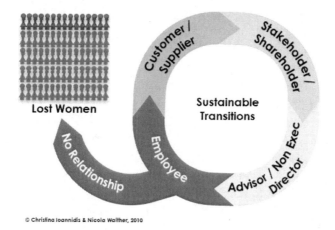

© Christina Ioannidis & Nicola Walther, 2010

Diagram 6: Sustainable Transitions

Today, companies find themselves in the left hand side of the image above. At the most important part of their careers, women are having to leave the corporate world, resulting in the female exodus most corporates experience at mid-management level.

In our survey 58% side-stepped at the main intersection of middle to senior management. However, if organisations take a long-term view of finding ways to build life-long relationships with their talent at that point, then women are likely to be drawn back to their particular organisation. What can be done to draw them back as potential customers or suppliers or even future employees? Ask:

> What can we do to keep our company as part of your life?

> If something is not working, how can you help us fix it? (This is an open, honest way to re-engage and offer them an opportunity to make a difference.)

The success of Semco, Brazil's fastest growing company, rests on having implemented such a truly sustainable model for maintaining employees throughout the transitions of their lives. Employees are encouraged to create their own companies and sell their time to the organisation as consultants. According to the CEO, this transparency and flexibility, has 'set many people free and opened entirely new horizons for others'[liv].

Janet Hanson, a former Goldman Sachs executive and the founder of the global network 85 Broads commented, 'Corporations can learn a lot from their employees who leave to become entrepreneurs if they are smart enough to treat them as alumni and not just as former employees. After I left Goldman Sachs in 1993, I returned in 1995 as a client of the firm. The smartest firms on the planet truly understand how important it is to stay connected to former employees who may be a lucrative source of business after they exit the building.'

Once they are re-engaged, they become a stakeholder in the organisation – an interested party in its development, be it as a supplier, or as a customer. Keeping the relationship open also allows organisations to build those women into their talent pipeline for advisory positions and ultimately, board positions.

Truly supportive companies take a long-term position and maintain a relationship vis-à-vis their employees, so that if they leave the organisation, they are treated as alumni, as stakeholders.

As one of our respondents, a former investment banker, commented, 'Frankly, banks, as well as focusing on how to retain women, should be thinking about extending credit such that these successful female entrepreneurs will be banking with them.'

Sustainability and Generation Y

The themes we have discussed above correspond with the preoccupations of Generation Y. The Cone survey above illustrated the similarities very well. In addition to this, the London-based Centre for Women in Business recently published a study on this generation[lv]. They have been termed by the Centre for Women in Business as the 'reflexive' generation;

- This generation is constantly reflecting back on the relationship between self, work and life (strikingly similar to women's reflections)

- They believe they have to adapt constantly to achieve what they want in life
- This generation grew up at a time when jobs ceased to be 'for life' and the world shrank to become a 'global village'
- They have an appetite for new skills and want to work on engaging projects to maintain their momentum of motivation
- Diversity is accepted as normal and does not need to be stressed.

One of the overriding impressions of the men and women of this generation is their frustration with performance management practices which are too slow, bureaucratic and hierarchical. They want to learn fast and to change tack with elegance. To do this they need frequent feedback and more support and mentoring.

The Centre for Women in Business says that Generation Y comprises 'digital natives…who collaborate globally to create collaborative environments that benefit a much wider community than their own.' Interestingly, one of the more significant findings for the study was the 'design of work – they place a great deal of emphasis on "intellectual capital" (the knowledge and insights they have), social capital (the depth, richness and extent of their networks) and emotional capital (the means by which they understand themselves and build self-knowledge). For this generation the emphasis is "work to learn" rather than "work to live".'

A pertinent factor common to both women and Generation Y, is the desire to give back to the community through work. This altruistic, ethically driven stance represents an increasingly vocal shift openly to require corporations to support and develop the community, even heal the planet.

Encouraging skills and personal development programmes in organisations revolving around social and community activities close to employees' hearts is important for this group. These should be incorporated as part of their personal development plans, not as activities to be undertaken outside office hours.

Conclusion

Numerous studies have highlighted that managing diversity in a sustainable fashion is important in winning the war over talent – attracting, retaining and creating long-term value from the toughest customers: their toughest employees. In this chapter we maintain that creating a sustainable talent management attitude also satisfies the added requirement of managing the new generation, Generation Y.

The similarities between what motivates women and what motivates Generation Y as a group are clear. We also found that truly to embrace diversity in business the following words from the London Centre for Women in Business study, resonate powerfully and concur with our thinking:

'... the wise executive will understand that flexibility is not a women issue – it is an issue beyond gender to the core of what it is to be human... Work life is a marathon – not a sprint – and like a marathon it needs to contain pacing, stamina and resilience.'

Section 2: Gender-Savvy in Practice

Chapter 6: Gender and Marketing

We decided to dedicate a chapter to this topic to highlight how strategically important gender diversity is for businesses and to demonstrate how our model can work in the marketing context. If talent is your greatest resource and fishing from half the pool is a strategic mistake, then targeting less than half of the potential customers is an even bigger strategic error. This chapter shows how the principles in this book can be utilised to put the diversity agenda at the centre of strategic planning.

While Human Resources has a major strategic role in some enlightened businesses, we have heard too many times during our research how businesses have passed the buck on diversity to HR. We have already explained in chapter 2, how ensuring retention of the best talent to create, design and deliver products and services should not be left to one single department. Anyone who has been in a senior position in a business will understand that leaving an issue of strategic importance to one department in isolation is folly.

According to Bain and Co, men and women equally believe that gender diversity is a requirement in business[lvi]. However, only '48% of men feel that achieving gender parity should be a critical business imperative for their organisations.' In this chapter, we will highlight how diversity of thought is key to opening the future prospects of an organisation.

Why is gender diversity important in marketing?

Marti Barletta, author of *Marketing to Women*, says, 'In many respects women want all the same things as men – and then some. Accordingly, when you meet the higher expectations of women, you are more than fulfilling the demands of men. You've got two satisfied customers for the price of one, so which market would you emphasise?'

Markets are saturated. Business needs constantly to devise, create and deliver cleverly targeted products and services. Moreover, consumers are bombarded with millions of other marketing messages every day. If a company is to guarantee longevity, it should be in tune with what its customers want. As we saw in Chapter 1 above, women hold the purse-strings in all industries, ranging from the stereotypically male automotive, financial services and healthcare through to consumer goods and beauty products.

McKinsey and Co analysed 89 European listed companies with the highest level of gender diversity in top management posts. The companies were selected from all European listed companies with a stock market capitalisation of over €150 million, on the basis of the following criteria: the number and proportion of women on the executive committee, their function (a CEO or CFO having greater weight in corporate decisions than a Communications Manager) and the presence of more than two women on the board, and statistics on gender diversity in the annual report. McKinsey then analysed the financial performance of these companies relative to the average for their sector. They concluded that there can be no doubt that, on average, these companies outperformed their sector in terms of:

> Return on equity (11.4% vs an average 10.3%),
>
> Operating result (EBIT 11.1% vs 5.8%),
>
> Stock price growth (64% vs 47% over the period 2005-2007) [lvii]

If there are no women in senior strategic roles within the organisation, how can it identify the services, products, attributes and communication which can unlock the untapped female market? The door to the technical areas of an organisation, such as operations, logistics and product development, tends to be firmly shut to women, and what is beyond it is likely to be a male-dominated environment.

We invite leaders to ask themselves how many all-male meetings they have attended? In fact, perhaps they should make a record of meetings at which women are in attendance. At how many meetings were women represented by one woman, the only woman present? What role did the woman play in the meeting? Now consider, how many meetings included a minimum 50-50 gender split? If a business is to tap into the next growth economy, women must be making decisions and making recommendations rather than being relegated to support roles.

Gender-Savvy Value Chain Management

Below we examine some areas of value chain management and how they may be affected by the needs of female consumers. Each link of the value chain needs to address female customers' needs and the role that link performs in meeting the challenges posed by her work, family, and home responsibilities.

Product development and commercialisation

Marketing time can be reduced if customers and suppliers are integrated with the product development process. As product lifecycles shorten, the appropriate products must be developed and successfully launched with ever shorter schedules to remain competitive and dominate the market.

How does the product development department co-ordinate with customer relationship management teams to identify customer-articulated needs? For example, how would a product developer acquire first-hand information on what the targeted female segment needs?

How can just-in-time product development be ensured and a product and service lifecycle suitable for women be maintained?

How does the product add value throughout the personal and physical transformations – biological, financial and socially obligatory – women endure in their life?

How will those who understand the real life issues be talked to?

For example, the founder of a retailer selling maternity and baby products gave a speech at a conference we attended. She described one of her first products which was a complete failure; a maternity cat suit. She had never been pregnant and the garment looked great on paper but it didn't sell because (a) most pregnant women don't particularly want to show themselves in a cat suit and (b) pregnant women need to pee so often that a cat suit is extremely impractical!

Inbound Logistics / Procurement

How can a diversity of suppliers, offering a correspondingly diverse range of goods to present to demanding female customers, be guaranteed?

Outbound Logistics

What is the speed of delivery of products?

Are (female) customers given a choice of drop-off points so that delivery is at the customer's convenience and if she is working shifts or in multiple locations these can be accommodated?

What about delivery time-frames? Are deliveries only made between 9 and 5, so that the woman has to work from home or limit her caring activities to the house to ensure the delivery can be received?

Service

How are customers engaged with through the Web and other channels?

Is there a customer-response pledge? How is it controlled? Is it visible to customers?

What are the processes for registering a complaint?

Do female customers tell you about any 'extraordinary' requirements they may have from your proposition?

Does the customer service team have the capability to telephone back, so customers are not kept on hold for five or ten minutes (which is a major challenge when looking after an energetic 2-year-old....)?

Marketing and sales

Does a product or service indicate that it was designed with women in mind?

Is there direct, authentic dialogue with the customer, and is it free of negatively stereotyped assumptions?

Are intermediaries or third party sales-teams used to sell to consumers and to the female market?

How can the business extend the product or service lifecycle targeted at women? Can renewed or additional services be offered as her needs evolve?

Do you need to partner with complementary products to offer time-saving propositions to satisfy the time-pressured women?

Will this partnership extend to all sub-segments of the female market?

The answers to these questions may demonstrate where there are blind-spots in the organisation's consideration of the gender blend of the business and its capacity to service the female market. When an organisation is gender-proofed, it can cater to the most demanding customers and future business success is protected. What is needed to achieve that? The sections below offer our main strategies.

Focus on life-long customer value (rather than short-term profitability)

Traditional performance indicators are not the best measure of success when targeting the female market. When women are happy customers, they are also immensely loyal. Gaining their loyalty requires up-front investment and maintaining their loyalty requires ongoing customer service. We explain how to interact effectively with female customers below. Changing the corporate metrics to measure performance over the longer term may well take a shift in attitude, but we suggest it is worth while. Women are willing to pay a premium for products and services which release them from their time-pressure-cooker.

Gender-Savvy Customer Management

Integrate women and solve problems with them

Some of the areas covered in the value chain management example above show how structural bias may hold business back. The only way to redress that bias is to include more women in all areas of the business.

As we saw in the previous chapter, organisations can use the CLICs model to incorporate women in parts of the business where women may not, for a variety of reasons, be represented. In the short term, these gaps may be filled, when developing products for women, by engaging with women clients to ask them what they want.

Here are some ways of speaking directly to them:

> Ask for her opinion and value her individual input on products and service proposition.

> Intimacy rules. Forget focus groups. Have women round a table for dinner and listen. Ask pertinent questions but do not block the 'flow'.

> Be Creative: Don't disregard any ideas – encourage women to come up with solutions that work for them.

Make spokeswomen. Women love to learn as we saw in Chapter 2, so involve one of them with an activity by asking her to investigate what her friends may be thinking. Convert her into a real-life Miss Marple!

In the long term, such an organic approach will promote a culture change, embracing diversity of thought, as discussed in Chapter 4. The company will avoid negative stereotyping and is on the road to creating gender-smart products and services.

Box 6: Home Depot Canada Case Study

Home Depot Canada has taken one of the most significant steps towards reaching the female market. Under the tenure of the company's president, Annette Verschuren, the retail chain grew from 19 stores with $700m annual sales to 167 stores with revenues in excess of $6bn. Women constitute over 50% of purchasers in the stores today. To achieve this mammoth growth, Verschuren had to effect a major culture change. 'I knew women were hugely involved in home renovations and yet the female side of our business was seriously under-represented.'[lviii].

Verschuren took the following steps:

- Increased the number of women working in the business: Home Depot boasts the highest percentage of women merchants and buyers in the industry.

- Embarked on a culture change programme internally: she introduced gender-intelligent training and processes across the lines of business. She recruited diversity-focused individuals who acted as her spokespeople. She gave women a voice in the boardroom and in the stores.

- Recognised female consumer differences: women wanted to be taken as seriously as men, but not treated like men. From the store layout to customer service, Verschuren introduced female-centric consumer experience offering holistic, time-saving solutions for women who control expenditure in the home improvement market.

Women behave in a similar way online and in the real world – observe and learn!

Much in the same way as a woman's life is represented by a mesh of many responsibilities of the home, office, and family, women dominate the networked virtual world.

Women connect, share and shape in the virtual world. We believe women's use of technology represents a micro-filter on their attitude to life. Women are task-tacklers: they want tools to help them accomplish their tasks and enhance their ability to pursue interests (in terms of using technology, they don't care what the device is, for example, provided it does what is needed).

Research has identified certain key areas in which women manage their lives.

> **Women are connected:** Women's use of technology and digital machines combines entertainment, organisation and connectivity in the home and office. According to Nielsen Mobile, 13.5 million women have adopted the business-born Smartphone. (The number of users has doubled in the last two years).

Women have no off-switch: Women report using different devices (mobile phone, computer, TV, DVD etc) to perform multiple tasks and slot them into their activity list, irrespective of the time of day.

Women Share: Women are the best brand evangelists. Women have taken the 'Blogosphere to the Stratosphere':

> 36 million women write blogs weekly

> 50% of women believe that blogs are reliable sources for information[lix]

These blogs act as a platform for sharing the best and worst experiences, both in terms of personal, but also brand-related, experiences. Women's innate programming for emotional connection with others guides them to harness the power of technology to bring their passions (and frustrations) to the rest of the world. This is echoed by research undertaken by *People* magazine. Women are not only more likely than men to ask for opinions from friends, family, colleagues and their circle of contacts, they are also more likely to volunteer accounts of both good and bad purchase experiences. 79% of women have recommended three or more products in the past 12 months; 57% have recommended five or more products.

As the marketing guru Marti Barletta comments, 'Because they've done more homework upfront, [women] feel more confident recommending their choices to friends and others. … When you convert a male prospect into a male customer, you get a new male customer. When you convert a female prospect, you get more: not only her own greater purchasing role but also a life-long string of referrals[lx].

Women have no boundaries: The lines between work, family and 'her' time are blurred – she is accessible 24/7. This blurring is even more pronounced for women who are mothers. In the US, 84% of new mums research products online; this is more than the national average of 78%. 82% of new mums purchase products online[lxi] .

These themes resonate with women's attitudes to work too, as we saw in the previous chapters. Women need products which offer solutions or stimulate aspirations to make their challenged lives easier.

Use Technology to extend brand appeal to women

A product should not be limited to what it is today and packaged in pink in the hope it will be a hit with female consumers. One of the best mechanisms to broaden a range of services is with the power of technology to offer just-in-time products or services catering to women's multiple needs.

As Michael Silverstein and Kate Sayre of the Boston Consulting Group say, 'The triple challenge of time – and the stress and anxiety it can create – colors virtually everything women do. Products and services that can "give time back to them" are seen positively. Good products act as agents that enable women to make the most of time, regain more of it, and spend it as they want to, rather than as they have to. Products that require them to spend time in ways they don't want, or seen as unnecessary are villains. Goods that squeeze the most out of time – by making it more engaging for them personally or by enabling them to connect with others more deeply – are especially valued.'[lxii]

Re-examine the company's value chain and consider how technology can enable the presentation of simpler products, faster and more easily to women. Consider the simple ways that technology can assist with delivering time-sensitive and valuable services to women.

Here are some examples:

A mobile phone operator can offer a phone set-up consultation in their shop with new mothers or time-poor women where they install the most-time-saving applications in the customers' phones for them.

A hotelier can establish an automated check-out whereby rooms are cleaned in order of being vacated, so that some guests can stay longer than the 12 noon limit (and give them the chance to enjoy the establishment's amenities).

A financial services provider can stay in touch with her and ensure she has everything she needs in moving her business and personal accounts, with direct line access to a single individual in the firm with whom she can arrange appointments via text message.

Use the Gender-Savvy Model to build authentic relationships with customers

Women represent a powerful marketing machine and they have the ability to become a company's spokesperson. As we saw from Chapter 5, female employees can also be the greatest brand advocates, as long as the company and its products support them in their life transitions. From a simple purchaser she can become a brand ambassador by simply delighting her, offering her service, but also surpassing her expectations.

Box 7: Dove Case Study: The Virtual meets Reality

The Unilever product, Dove, has been a leading product for the organisation since 1979. In 2001 the moisturising soap had more than 24% market share. In 2004, Dove launched a new advertising campaign which attacked mainstream media and traditional advertising for their misinterpretation of the image of women[lxiii]. Dove set out to change the stereotype of female beauty by launching the 'Campaign for Real Beauty', with advertising that speaks directly to women of all ages and body types. The company's success lies in having carefully gender-proofed its proposition. Here we use our Gender-Savvy Model to demonstrate this:

Passion: the campaign spoke to women about their authentic selves, about their natural beauty.

Flexibility: women were asked to write letters to their own bodies, helping them embrace the variety, and even the beauty, that came with the imperfections of their own bodies in contrast to a manufactured image of beauty.

Collaboration: the company worked with women to define the campaign. It developed viral web strategies through a series of short films chiding the beauty industry – saying out loud what women were thinking. The brand included a website section on being 'pro-age' and spreading self-esteem among young girls. 13 articles of the Letters to your Body were even adapted into a stage play, with the winning writers in the leading roles, called *Body and Soul*. The short film, *Evolution*, exploring how the image of beauty has become distorted has had over 13 million hits on YouTube.

Sustainability: Dove launched the Dove Self-Esteem Fund organisation to fund self-esteem programmes for girls.

Consumers are active fundraisers and contact the company daily with ideas to raise funds for its activities.

The company has experienced double-digit growth every year since the launch of the 'Real Beauty' campaign – in a category that grows 2-3 percent annually – and annual sales now top $3 billion globally, making this the number one-selling cleanser in the world[lxiv].

We offer our Gender-Savvy model as a framework to tap into the largest market in the world, the female market. Here are some of the main considerations when designing products and services for the most demanding customers:

Passion
- How does your product help to tap into something that is close to her heart; something that she cares about?
- How engaging is your sales process? Does it offer a multi-sensory experience?
- Does your service or sales process enable her to learn something new about herself?
- How can she ask for more information? Is it possible to have a lengthy dialogue with a salesperson before purchase?
- Does your company brand communicate and deliver passion first hand?
- Do each one of your customer touch-points communicate the passion for what they do to customers? How precisely do they do that?

Flexibility
- What is the specific logistical problem your product or service is solving for her?
- Is your product or service easy to use?
- How are you making her life easier?
- Do you make it clear she is in the driving seat in the design of the product?
- How are you giving her an opportunity to voice her needs?
- Does she have the opportunity to think and come back to your sales-team before purchase?
- Do you give her options to choose from in terms of service?
- How far are your service delivery platforms synched up – web, mobile, telephone? Are you using them appropriately to offer pre- and post-sales services required?

Collaboration
- How do you involve her in the design process?
- How do you know what success you have had with other users? Do you have testimonials?
- At what point can she engage in dialogue with your product/service development teams?
- Have you engaged with other brands or channels to deliver a true ease-of-life product or service she cannot find elsewhere?
- How does your product extend its relevance into her needs through her life transitions?

Sustainability
- How does your product or service enable her to stay connected with her circle of influence?
- How can her contacts become involved in the purchase process?
- How can her contacts also benefit from the product/service or part of the sales process? (Word of mouth, bulk discount, etc)
- How can she share the outcome of her experiences with you with her friends and family?
- What are you going to offer her as a token of appreciation in return for doing that?

Deal with female customers as though they are the first ever customer. Imagine you are an entrepreneur wanting to please your first customers. Pull out all the stops. Deliver the corporate muscle with entrepreneurial, innovative yet gender-proofed flair.

Conclusion

If an organisation wants to tap into key purchase motivators for women, then it must engage women who understand and appreciate a female mind-set and can find ways to differentiate products to conquer the world's largest market: the stiletto dollar! Harness female views right across the organisation so that they can exert their insight and power in creating long-term product and service differentiators.

Chapter 7: Personal Development

'If your relationship with your manager is fractured, then no amount of in-chair massaging or company sponsored dog walking will persuade you to stay and perform. It is better to work for a great manager in an old-fashioned company than for a terrible manager in a company offering enlightened, employee-focused culture.' Marcus Buckingham and Curt Coffman[lxv]

Stop fixing the women

Multiple studies, particularly those undertaken by the leading research company, Gallup, have shown that when employees leave companies, they are leaving managers. It is often a lack of personal support or problems with direct line management which most upset employees and are the most common reasons for departure.

This lack of sympathy is even more critical in the case of women, who feel less well understood and involved in the business, owing to behavioural differences between the genders, manifested in the company culture. Two of our respondents commented as follows when asked what companies could do to retain more women: '1. Let women grow, do not subjugate them. 2. Give them a chance to take decisions, respect their decisions. 3. Understand that women are also as ambitious as men and they are serious about what ever they do'... 'Change the culture so that performance management is output-based rather than face-time based. Greatly increase the level of communication so that HR policies and the real culture is actually aligned.'

This chapter is designed for managers who want to grow the female talent in their organisations. It shows how the manager can act in a supportive way to help foster an inclusive, gender-proofed management style, but also how the women who want to take control can navigate their careers in male-dominated environments.

What women want from their leaders

Our research has highlighted the following behavioural traits as appealing to women:

Be Personal

Although women are multi-taskers, when they are talking with a colleague or friend, they devote all their attention to it. Their empathic brain concentrates on the issue at hand, and all other activities take second place. They focus their attention on listening, taking in and acknowledging what their counterpart is saying. This is what women expect from their leaders. In discussion with her about her future, her performance or her projects, focus exclusively on her. No emails, no texts nor third-party requests are acceptable at this time. The manager's eyes and ears need to be turned towards her.

This is also particularly important with an employee who is facing the dreaded maternity discussion. This is one of the greatest management challenges for both sides. Traditionally, men don't feel at ease discussing the m-word, or they laugh it off with flippant comments such as, 'Don't expect your job to be waiting for you when you get back.' For the woman, the fear of this sort of reaction, unhelpful and unfriendly, as if she has done something terrible, is compounded by her feeling of guilt at her perceived professional suicide by having children.

Box 8: Managing Maternity Case Study

An interviewee from an Australian Bank, was delighted with how the organisation managed the maternity process for her. This is what she recounted in the interview:

The process was handled from beginning to end; it was very structured. 'This is what you need to do, complete this form.' Even though I originally thought I would be back in 6 months I actually ended up taking 9 months off. At no point in my 9 months off did I not feel part of the company. There were a number of times when the company stayed in touch with me. The company sends a Thank you every 12 months to their staff, and they fly them to Sydney to have an event, and that's the company's way of saying 'Thank You very much we appreciate your efforts for the last 12 months.' As I was on maternity leave and unable to attend, they actually sent me a voucher for a few dollars and said, 'Sorry you are unable to attend but we really appreciate your contribution to the team – happy shopping.' And that note was hand written from our CEO – which was lovely!

Managers need to be proactive, but in a soft way, so that they let a person know they are still a valued member of the team...without exerting any pressure. Perhaps it is just a phone call to say, 'Hi, how are you doing?' You don't want contact for absolutely no reason – but if there is a reason and a positive reason then touch base. My boss rang me to tell me, 'You will receive a credit in your next salary of this amount...' – he could have just let that go and let me receive the letter saying that 'We are crediting you this'... but he chose to be proactive as well and actually picked up the phone – that was really nice but not too much. I think the reason for maternity leave is that there are big challenges for women to adapt to, so it was good to have that break. I had nine months off and if I heard from them once a quarter then that was fine, I didn't need to be hearing every week or every month.

In managing the transition back from maternity into the organisation, she would advise managers to:

Share a pre-vision of what (their direct reports) are coming back to and what the expectations are – to have a clear understanding and clear vision of your role upon return. It is good if this was a relaxed chat, an informal coffee or a meeting saying, 'Hey, this is what I am thinking...'

I think mentally you can prepare as well. If you turn up on day one not knowing what the expectations are it is very stressful; and along with the stress of leaving your child or children behind and you are concerned and don't know what you are going back to. And for some people this may make a big impact on their decision on whether they are going to return to work or if they don't.

The devil is in the detail – be structured

Women are able to commit much to memory. They recall with great precision the words, actions, and even non-verbal signals that their male colleagues give out. It is important for managers to remember exactly what they agreed to in discussions and to act on what they will say you will do. Managers should be structured in approaching conversations: keep a log, take notes and record clearly set actions and time-frames.

Offer constructive feedback and recognition

Women are programmed to speak their minds with discretion. While they seek feedback, they are sensitive to the way it is delivered. If feedback is not constructive, they wonder what is wrong rather than focusing on what specifically needs to be worked on or improved. If something can be done better or more effectively, tell her. In general terms, women are very practical and would rather 'have the truth'. Recognise her efforts too. Congratulate her for a job well done or an achievement gained. Even a small thank you can go a long way. On average, women need more recognition than men, from our experience, as much as three times more than men!

Be the Change...

The leader who asks their team to challenge itself must be able to meet the challenge him or herself. As Gandhi famously said, 'Be the change you want to see in the world'. The leader needs to be a walking role-model of the behaviour which women, and Generation Y, will respect. They will appreciate their leader's being involved in philanthropic schemes, as part of his or her own personal development plan, or using mentoring programmes to understand the innovative capabilities of entrepreneurs who can be learned from. Demonstrating support for such activities will earn respect and gratitude from the team.

Walking the Talk: Becoming a Gender-Savvy leader

In Chapter 3 we outlined what a business needs to do from a talent management perspective to dismantle stereotypical attitudes and support women's advancement within large corporations. In this chapter, we will reveal what some of the women who have left the corporate sphere have said. We explain how to foster an environment which engages women so that they stay loyal to the organisation throughout their career transitions.

Gender-Savvy Checklist

We have designed this as a self-questioning tool. Managers and leaders already have basic management skills. Based on the research and data, we have created this checklist of actions to encourage teams to recognise behaviours that will enable leaders to engage in long-term, mutually enhancing relationships with the most demanding (female) employees.

Igniting Passions

This is about winning hearts, about the strategies which can be implemented to tune in to a female employees' passions:

- How far have you asked your employees what they want from their careers?
- Do you know what success look like for your employees?
- How far are they doing what they want and enjoy, i.e., what they are passionate about?
- Have you appointed an Engagement Champion to ensure their development is focused on working on what they are good at, and passionate about?
- Have you set a clear Personal Engagement Plan?
- What mechanisms have you put in place to ensure learning can take place 'on the job'?
- Have you set up a Mentoring Programme to cross-fertilise thinking between your organisation and other companies?
- When did you reward them for their last achievement? When was the last time you said a simple 'thank you' for a great job?
- When did you last review their activities and achievements? Have you set (and adhered to) specific review dates?
- How structured have you been in your review meetings?

Fostering Flexibility

Fostering flexibility will make a happy trinity of work, home and family. Each employee is likely to need a different approach, but processes can be created to engage in dialogue and proactively support her need to be efficient and effective in all areas of her life.

- How far have you and your female team members spoken openly about their career trajectories?

Where do they see taking some reduced responsibility as necessary, or reduced travel? Make sure you ask them rather than making assumptions – start the dialogue and listen.

- What demands are you making in terms of employees performing their professional tasks – does a particular employee really have to be in the office at all times?
- Are there different ways in which responsibilities can be taken, for example, working away from the office or via flexible timings (e.g., working in 'shifts') or even shared with someone else?
- Have you asked the employee directly how this can be done? The employee is empowered by implementing her ideas.
- How do you check that one employee's performance is not being hampered by other individuals who have a different attitude to work-life balance and presenteeism? Have you spoken to these others about their assessments on her performance?
- How can you actively support an employee to extend her personal visibility?
- Who in the business can help her grow and give her exposure to areas of which you may not have direct knowledge? (Step right up, the Engagement Champion!)
- How can you help her create her Mentoring Mesh – her individual board of directors?
- To what extent do you have a set approach to changes in career development? How far are you enabling an employee to challenge herself in new

areas and enhance her business skills? Can you sponsor a project which gives her such learning, as well as visibility?

- Do you recognise that while an employee may not have direct experience in a particular role, she possesses skills that can help her perform what is required in a new role or project she may be interested in?

- How will you support her if she takes a risk and fails? How will you ensure she is not stigmatised by the rest of the organisation if an activity is not successful?

Cultivating Collaboration

This is about fuelling an employee's, and the company's, innovation tanks by encouraging her to offer solutions to specific problems. Create internal hubs of innovation to investigate, build, review the company's products, services and even its working culture:

- How is an employee using her natural creative flair in the business?

- Have you actively supported any activities she likes to undertake, which may not be an official part of her daily routine, but which can enhance her personal development?

- How can you incorporate this experience as part of her personal development plan?

- In what ways are you supporting her to implement changes internally that may work for the organisation?

- How are you helping her drive innovation internally? Are there ways in which she can make a difference to the business in uncharted areas?
- What collaborative working tools and processes are you installing to stimulate cross-fertilisation of ideas and thinking between her and other staff?
- How is an employee engaged in high-visibility projects which can challenge her and enhance her learning?
- How are you incorporating the CLIC model to engage in developing female-targeted products and services with clients and customers?

Supporting Sustainability

Communicating the soul of the business, inside and outside the organisation

- Which charitable causes do your female employees care about?
- How can they be incorporated as part of your marketing or service proposition?
- How can you support both in-office and out-of-office activities your female employees want to undertake in any charitable organisation?
- Who needs to be aware of the work and deliverables, which demonstrate true business skills, they may be contributing to charitable organisations?
- How can you utilise this commercial experience in the area of corporate social responsibility as part of their personal development plans?
- How are you supporting them in communicating their achievements and added value in quantifiable

terms (e.g., increase in revenue, cost savings to the business, etc) to the rest of the organisation?

- Which other stakeholder from within, and outside the business, may be interested in becoming involved in such activities? How will you open the dialogue with them?

Breaking Gender Stereotypes

Leaders can use the tool above as a management mechanism for women, Generation Y and men. Companies which have started activities to support (gender) diversity witnessed cultural improvements for all populations within and outside their organisations. The European Commission records that diversity programmes[lxvi] have had a positive impact on employee motivation for 58% of companies which implemented them. They have also witnessed:

> 57% improved customer satisfaction and

> 69% noted an improvement in brand image

We invite our readers to use this tool freely in harnessing individual employees' strengths and contributions, and break gender stereotypes.

Women, wake up!

We have spent the majority of this book giving advice to leaders and managers. It seemed fitting that we should remind the female readers of a few home truths as well. The organisations and their leadership cannot be expected to do this by themselves.

Women working in large corporations may feel isolated at times. They may feel at odds with their career aspirations, their family and home responsibilities. They may even feel at odds with their employer and the prevailing culture at work, as some of our respondents and interviewees commented in the previous chapters. All the evidence in this book and our qualitative and quantitative research will have given readers an idea of what women have wanted but not experienced in dealing with their corporate employers.

The women who participated in our research are now successfully pursuing their passions. To do that, they have taken control of their destiny and their future. They have made the leap of faith into new business ventures and either become entrepreneurs or are running a portfolio career. We have written this part of the book for employees, to guide them through some of the hard questions they should be asking themselves as they manage their careers. Emily Walker, corporate executive turned entrepreneur gave us some advice:

'Believing someone else is going to take care of you is really risky. As a woman I recommend that you should always be able to take care of yourself. If you are a mother, make sure that you can take care of your kids because, in the end, you can count on no one else but yourself.'

All the women we spoke to adhered to three main tenets for taking control and this is our advice for women on managing their own careers:

1. Be proactive

Women tend to focus on being excellent at what they do and feel a sense of duty to deliver and offer support to all around. They work away unnoticed, driving themselves into the ground and, of course, are disappointed when they cannot fulfill everyone's, and most importantly, their own very high, expectations. We invite you to be proactive about your career. Focus on what you need, on what will give you more time, more attention to what you are good at and a greater challenge. Don't despair.

2. Have courage: Speak out! Be succinct!

Women are great workers. They are the silent holders of the fort. While men are keen networkers, women believe 'my work will speak for itself'. We have news for you: it very seldom does. You must reject what you learned at school or at home that 'girls should not brag or speak out'. If you don't talk about your successes, who will? If you do not voice your discontent, how will your manager or organisation know the challenges you are facing? We applaud the women who start women's networks and other such affinity groups because, at the very least, they have brought to the discussion the culture in which women find themselves and the challenges they face. Keep what you say brief and to the point, say what you, not 'we', the team, did. Have the courage to ask for what you are worth, 'I contribute X,Y and Z to the business. I would expect A in return.' If your line manager or sponsor will not listen, move on. Enlightened organisations will react and will support you. If they don't, they simply do not deserve you. You can then move on, with no love lost.

3. Be outwardly focused

Women tend to be focused on their own working environment and are excellent internal networkers. The common assumption is that your employers will look after you, but in changing times, or when redundancy occurs, the absence of a good external network is keenly felt. You must build external networks to ease your transition to pastures new. We have helped hundreds of women to be strategic in building networks, within and outside their organisations. You need to build that network and promote your own, strong personal brand around your area of expertise.

As Emily Walker's quote above suggests, if you want recognition, flexibility and to 'feel' engaged with your work but also able to fulfil your family obligations, you and only you can do this. We invite you to consider the following framework to think of yourself and your career as an entrepreneur would of their business.

Portray Passion
- Identify what you do best – spend 80% of your time doing just that!
- Create you personal brand for what you do best, and enjoy doing
- Promote your contribution to the business, both in monetary terms and with ENERGY. Quite simply, energy sells!

- Passionately believe in yourself – people are fascinated by passion – because lack of confidence is interpreted as low self-esteem and so is likely to undermine your credibility
- Focus on your transferable skills. Demonstrate resilience by managing difficult tasks and changes. Post credit-crunch, resilience is seen as a most valued leadership trait
- Become an expert: develop an invaluable skill-set for the business, a reason why you are indispensable. Keep your personal achievement logs, your CV, blogs, etc, up to date

Find Flexibility

- Incorporate flexibility in your career: seek out roles which give you strategic, big-picture perspective. Work across departments and industries
- Work with others: outside those in your circle of influence
- If you have to take a side move, off /on ramp, prepare and create your personal visibility plan: don't lose touch; keep stakeholders updated with your achievements (even if you don't think they are achievements!). Remember the old adage: out of sight is out of mind
- Develop your Mentoring Mesh, your suite of board of directors; convert them to become your brand evangelists!

Connect Collaboratively

- Network strategically: look beyond your existing network of contacts. Embrace social media tools such as LinkedIn, Twitter to get you 'out there'
- Offer to help and support others – even upwards; line managers and senior managers are people too, after all, and they need skilled support
- Create your own brand evangelists: find ways to collaborate with men and women outside your current area of involvement. This helps to promote what you do, and vice versa
- Bring back new ideas to your business, and find ways to implement them. Today's success is about speed and performance to save costs and increase revenue, so anything you can do to achieve that will get management attention
- Constantly open new doors: find ways to work and learn across industries and locations
- Use all the social media tools available to you. Promote what you do and your contribution as if you were a company: Brand You plc!
- Create a brand development buddy so you have your support group in times of transition, someone you trust and who offers sound advice
- Set up your own career development group to push you in a new direction and to be your sounding board when things get sticky for you.

Support Sustainability

- Use your altruism to become involved in a project or charitable activity you are passionate about. Volunteer, or even better, join an advisory committee on a non-executive basis. Also, remember that trustees of charities tend to be influential people!

- Make a virtuous circle of renewal: keep refreshing your support group so that your contacts don't go stale
- Publicise the projects you are involved in. Other stakeholders will be interested. These individuals will not only help you to get your message out there but they are also good for your business (and your career)
- If you are happy where you are working, recommend friends to your employer to work with you. Research proves that the more friends individuals have at work, the greater their sense of engagement *and* they are likely to be your consistent, long-term supporters!

Personal branding is beyond the scope of this book but readers will have noted that it is a common thread in the model above. If you don't already have a strong idea about your personal brand there are several good books on the subject. It is particularly important for a woman who is juggling multiple areas of her life, because she is bound to find conflict between expected behaviours in her work life and her home life. This needs to be balanced, because with personal branding the most important thing is: whatever you do and however you choose to do it, *be consistent* (which is easier to do if you are being true to yourself). You are what you repeatedly do. That is what gives brands their identity and what makes people believe in the real you.

For example, Tiger Woods's brand was badly damaged by his extra-marital affairs because he was held up as a paragon of virtue. What he did was inconsistent with his brand. Charlie Sheen, on the other hand, when essentially making very similar mistakes, didn't affect his brand at all. If anything, it strengthened his bad boy image!

You can download this personal assessment tool from: www.yourlossbook.com

Conclusion: Join the Revolution

In this part of the chapter we have touched upon the importance of women taking control of their career. We have drawn on our experience in working with women we coached and trained to succeed in challenging (and male-dominated) fields. We wanted this section to act as a wake-up call for women to take command of their destiny so that their professional and personal success is no longer entirely dependent on others. Only when women speak up on what they want will corporate and social cultures realise that they must meet these needs. For those who are managing women, expect and demand that they meet you half way by being proactive, speaking out and becoming more outwardly focused. As a manager, do your part by understanding what women want and use the self-questioning tool above to identify how you can walk the talk.

Welcome to the start of the corporate cultural revolution.

References

[i] Harvard Business Review, *The Female Economy*, September 2009

[ii] Tom Peters, foreword, *Marketing to Women* Marti Barletta, 2006, Dearborn Trade Publishing

[iii] Barclays Wealth Report, *A Question Of Gender*, 2006

[iv] Catalyst, *The Bottom Line, Connecting Corporate Performance and Gender Diversity*, 2004

[v] Roy Adler, *'Women in the Executive Suite Correlates to High Profits'* http://s3.amazonaws.com/mmc-beta-production/assets/11195/MMResearch_Essay.pdf

[vi] Harvard Business Review, *The Female Economy*, September 2009

[vii] Unesco, *Global Education Digest*, 2009

[viii] Center for Work-Life Policy, *Off Ramps and On Ramps Revisited*, 2009

[ix] Women's Institute for Policy Research, *Fact Sheet, 2010*

[x] UK Office For National Statistics, *Annual Survey of Earnings*, 2009

[xi] Maddy Dychtwald with Christine Larson, Influence, *How Women's Soaring Economic Power Will Transform Our World for the Better*, 2009, Voice (Hyperion)

[xii] Barclays Bank Press Release, *Business start-ups steady in 2008*, 25 March 2009

[xiii] London Business School, *Global Entrepreneurship Monitor*, February 2006

[xiv] Peters, Ryan, and Haslam, University of Exeter, *Fitting in or opting out: How perceptions of leadership impact on career ambition,* 2009.

[xv] Women & Men Business Owners in the United Kingdom, http://www.prowess.org.uk/facts.htm

[xvi] UK Small Business Service, *A Strategic Framework for Women's Enterprise,* 2003; http://www.prowess.org.uk/facts.htm

[xvii] British Chambers of Commerce, *Achieving the Vision, Female Entrepreneurship,* 2004

[xviii] London Business School, *Global Entrepreneurship Monitor,* February 2006

[xix] The Female Economy *Harvard Business Review,* September 2009

[xx] Avivah Wittenberg-Cox, *How Women mean Business,* 2010, Jossey-Bass (John Wiley & Sons Ltd)

[xxi] Tina Seelig, *What I wish I know when I was 20,* 2009, HarperCollins

[xxii] Margaret Henig and Anne Jardim, *The Managerial Woman,* 1976, Pocket Books

[xxiii] Center for Work-Life Policy, *The Hidden Brain Drain: Off-Ramps and On-ramps in Women's Careers,* 2005

[xxiv] Center for Work-Life Policy, *The Hidden Brain Drain: Off-Ramps and On-ramps in Women's Careers,* 2005

[xxv] answers.com, http://www.answers.com/topic/old-boy-network

[xxvi] Center for Work-Life Policy, *Off Ramps and On Ramps Revisited,* 2009

[xxvii] David Clutterback, *Everyone needs a Mentor, Fostering Talent in your Organisation,* 2004, Chartered Institute of Personnel and Development

[xxviii] Ricardo Semler, *The Seven-Day Weekend,* 2003, Arrow Books

[xxix] Center for Work-Life Policy, *Off Ramps and On Ramps Revisited,* 2009

[xxx] McKinsey and Co, *Women Matter, A Corporate Performance Driver,* 2007

[xxxi] DDI, *Holding Women Back,* A Special Report from DDI's Global Leadership Forecast 2008|2009

[xxxii] Fortune Magazine, *100 Best Companies to Work For,* 2007

[xxxiii] Catalyst, *Women 'Take Care', Men 'Take Charge'; Stereotyping of US Business Leaders Exposed,* 2005

[xxxiv] Press Release: Fatherhood Institute gives political parties six signposts to a better future for fatherhood

[xxxv] Gregory Berns, *Iconoclast,* 2008, Harvard Business Press

[xxxvi] Binna Kandola, *The Value of Difference,* 2009, Pearn Kandola Publishing

[xxxvii] PricewaterhouseCoopers Report, *The Leaking Pipeline,* 2007

[xxxviii] Gregory Berns, *Iconoclast,* 2008, Harvard Business Press

[xxxix] Binna Kandola, *The Value of Difference,* 2009, Pearn Kandola Publishing

[xl] Binna Kandola, *The Value of Difference,* 2009, Pearn Kandola Publishing

[xli] Ricardo Semler, *Maverick,* 1993, Arrow Books

[xlii] *Women and Work Survey*, Grazia Magazine, 2010

[xliii] McKinsey and Co, *Women Matter, A Corporate Performance Driver*, 2007

[xliv] Science Daily, *Collective Intelligence, Number of Women in Group Linked to Effectiveness in Solving Difficult Problems*, 2 October 2010, http://www.sciencedaily.com/releases/2010/09/10093 0143339.htm?ref=nf

[xlv] The Lehman Brothers Centre for Women in Business, *Innovative Potential, Men and Women in Teams*, November 2007

[xlvi] Teresa M. Amabile and Mukti Khaire, Harvard Business Review, *Creativity and the Role of the Leader*, 2008

[xlvii] Jeffrey Sanchez-Burks, Fiona Lee, University of Michigan, Ross School of Business, *Identity Integration and Innovation*, March 2007

[xlviii] Gregory Berns, *Iconoclast*, 2008

[xlix] Frans Johansson, *The Medici Effect*, 2004, Harvard Business School Publishing

[l] William C. Taylor, *Here's an Idea: Let Everyone Have Ideas*, New York Times, March 26, 2006

[li] Frans Johansson, *The Medici Effect*, 2004, Harvard Business School Publishing

[lii] The 2010 Cone Cause Evolution Study presents the findings of an online survey conducted July 29-30, 2010 by ORC among a demographically representative US sample of 1,057 adults comprising 512 men and 545 women 18 years of age and older. The margin of error associated with a sample of this size is ± 3%.

[liii] Cone, *Cause Evolution Study*, 2010,
ww.coneinc.com/whatdoyoustandfor

[liv] Ricardo Semler, *Maverick*, 1993, Arrow Books

[lv] London Business School, *The Reflexive Generation: Young Professionals' Perspectives on Work, Career and Gender*, 2009

[lvi] Julie Coffman, Orit Gadiesh and Wendy Miller, Bain and Co Report, *The Great Disappearing Act, Gender Parity up the Corporate Ladder*, 2010

[lvii] Mc Kinsey and Co, *Women Matter*, 2007

[lviii] Joanne Thomas Yaccato and Sean McSweeney, *The Gender Intelligent Retailer*, 2008, John Wiley and Sons Canada Ltd

[lix] Microsoft Advertising, Ogilvy & Mindshare, *Women in their Digital Domain*, June 2009

[lx] Marti Barletta *Marketing to Women*, 2006

[lxi] Microsoft Advertising, Ogilvy & Mindshare, *Women in their Digital Domain*, June 2009

[lxii] Michael J. Silverstein and Kate Sayre, *Women Want More*, 2009, HarperCollins

[lxiii] Michael J. Silverstein and Kate Sayre, *Women Want More*, 2009 HarperCollins

[lxiv] Michael J. Silverstein and Kate Sayre, *Women Want More*, 2009, HarperCollins

[lxv] Marcus Buckingham and Curt Coffman, *First, Break All the Rules*, 2005, Simon and Schuster

[lxvi] European Commission, *The Cost and Effectiveness of Diversity*, 2003